Finding Home

WRITTEN BY
Corinne Joy Brown

STORY BY
Corinne Joy Brown and
Ginny McDonald

ILLUSTRATED BY
Ginny McDonald

Loose Cayuse
PRODUCTIONS™

*Mustang-Inspired Literature
for Horse Lovers Everywhere*

Finding Home
Text Copyright © 2019 Corinne Joy Brown
Illustration Copyright © 2019 Ginny McDonald
All Rights Reserved.

Any similarity to actual persons or places (except for the Rock Springs Holding Facility) is unintended and coincidental.

No part of this book may be reproduced or transmitted in any form by any means, except for brief excerpts used in a review, without prior written permission from the copyright holder, which may be requested through the publisher.

Illustrations: Ginny McDonald
Cover and Interior Design: Rebecca Finkel, FPGD.com

ISBN paperback: 978-0-578-46964-5

Library of Congress Control Number: data on file

To all the wild horses everywhere and to the girls (and boys) who love them.

Contents

CHAPTER ONE	Pahaska	1
CHAPTER TWO	Capture	8
CHAPTER THREE	To Own a Horse	12
CHAPTER FOUR	Adoption	20
CHAPTER FIVE	Be Careful What You Wish For	24
CHAPTER SIX	A Tough Surprise	27
CHAPTER SEVEN	Rescue	31
CHAPTER EIGHT	Home on the Ranch	36
CHAPTER NINE	Becoming a Warrior	42
CHAPTER TEN	Waiting	50
CHAPTER ELEVEN	School Time	53
CHAPTER TWELVE	Homecoming	59
CHAPTER THIRTEEN	Breakout	63
CHAPTER FOURTEEN	On the Road Again	67
CHAPTER FIFTEEN	Is This Home?	73
CHAPTER SIXTEEN	Class Report	81
CHAPTER SEVENTEEN	The Full Report	85
CHAPTER EIGHTEEN	One Step at a Time	92
CHAPTER NINETEEN	Changing Gears	94
CHAPTER TWENTY	Working It Out	98
CHAPTER TWENTY-ONE	Wanderlust	101
CHAPTER TWENTY-TWO	The Next Challenge	105
CHAPTER TWENTY-THREE	Closing In	110

CHAPTER TWENTY-FOUR	On the Run	114
CHAPTER TWENTY-FIVE	Lost and Found	117
CHAPTER TWENTY-SIX	Guided by Instinct	123

About the Author 130

About the Illustrator 130

CHAPTER ONE

Pahaska

Dawn broke over the flatlands of Rock Springs, Wyoming, clear and cool, faint wisps of early morning clouds dissolving into the sun. My flaxen-maned mother, knowing she was approaching her time, left the herd by herself and lay down in a sandy, sheltered draw. It didn't take very long before I came along.

That special day, my birth-day, took place nearly three years ago. I was one of many foals born in the spring, before a long, arid summer; a time that changed the life of our small, wild herd forever. Like most newborn horses, I was on my feet within minutes and joined the others my age in the discovery of a brand new world—warm summer wind to caress our faces, fresh water rushing by, and a mother's milk whenever we wanted.

I remember how my mother's red, sorrel coat shone in the sun as she walked beside me. Her creamy mane and tail, a sharp contrast, made her easy to spot from a distance. For some reason her fine hair wasn't curly and thick like mine, but lay flat and smooth instead. In spite of my curls, she said I was the prettiest foal she'd ever had. Number four, I think, and a filly. (Yes, number four.) I liked it when she licked my face and neck, and my fuzzy coat turned to golden spirals all over. It felt good. My mother was my protector and my very best friend. I followed her closely over the next few days, weeks, and even months, learning what a young horse needed to know in order to survive in the wild.

༄

One morning, just a few years later, our band of mares and their offspring headed down a slope to the creek below. My mother trotted by me, the staccato of her hooves as familiar as my own. She carried a little brother or sister inside her at the time, soon to make its appearance. As long as she was near, I could always endure the crowding and pushing of other horses on either side. They were thirsty and so was I. After a refreshing long drink, we headed for the new grass growing along the banks, sweet and tender. Breakfast!

I was nostril-deep into my first bite when I heard the noise above, a roar louder than thunder. The wind around us stirred like a heavy summer storm with huge gusts tossing our manes, creating angry clouds of dust. I lowered my head and coughed, moving toward my mother's flank for safety. "What is it?" I called.

Before she could answer, the entire herd bolted, some heading back the way we'd come. Tecumseh, our battle-scarred stallion, took the lead and as old as he was, tried hard to stay in front and guide us all toward safety. I galloped as fast as my legs would carry me, determined not to lose sight of him or my mother's long, flaxen tail streaming ahead. Panic filled the air and something deep inside told me we were in trouble.

"Mother!" I whinnied, but she didn't look back. "Mother, wait for me…" I called again, losing ground as I watched her long legs carry her far ahead. The noisy, giant bird lowered itself over our heads and the herd began to turn.

"Wait!" I cried, stumbling, "We never go this way. Never!"

The earth below slid under our feet as we scrambled over an ancient gravel bed. Here and there a horse went down, slipping and falling to one side. Their terrified screams made me shudder as I ran. My heart pumping, I loped along and took my place in a long, ragged line of terrified horses racing together toward some unknown, hoped-for exit, until—slam! We could run no more.

The running herd had hit an enclosure, something I'd never seen before. We were quickly barricaded as something clanged behind us, closing us in. We started to mill, round and round, confused and frantic to get out. Everywhere I looked were walls we could see through, but couldn't pass through, no matter how hard we tried.

I don't know how, but a few remnants of our band had escaped the entrapment and thundered on past. Entire families were separated. Tecumseh, our leader, squeezed against the perimeter of our prison and began pacing its length. But worst of all, no matter where I looked, my beloved mother was nowhere to be seen.

Confused by the noise, the roundup, and the capture, I fell in with the others as they turned circles in a fury, separated from the life we had always known. After what seemed a very long time, I settled down, exhausted, and stood near the old stallion. Now and then, I raised my head hoping to catch sight of my mother, somewhere, anywhere.

"Mother," I whinnied, pricking my ears this way and that, hoping to hear her return my call. "Mother, where are you?" But she was clearly not among us. That was my very last attempt to reach her before we were forcibly pushed up a ramp and hustled into something long, narrow and tall. All the horses crowded against one another, many dazed in fear and trembling, as the thing we found ourselves in began to move. We were jostled and bumped, bracing our legs so we wouldn't fall down. After the big enclosure rolled through the canyon in clouds of dust, spitting out stones and gravel and spewing black smoke, it took us far away in to the fading afternoon, and on into the darkest night.

CHAPTER TWO

Capture

We awoke the next morning to a large pen where hundreds of horses were already assembled. They were strangers to me, herds I'd never seen before. Before long, two-legged creatures approached. ("Men" is what I learned they were called.) I had previously only seen them from afar. Sometimes they rode, sitting upon horses that actually allowed them on their backs. Sometimes they walked. At this moment, they approached on foot and threw large bundles of what looked like dead grass into our space. Then they retreated, watching us.

Hours passed and the day dragged on. I must have dozed. I woke up from my snooze to the clatter of hooves striking a metal barrier. It was my father, Shako, who had been herded into an adjacent pen. Furious, nostrils flaring, he struck again and again at the fence (I learned later that's what it was called), splintering the edges of his hooves and nicking his forelegs and hocks until they bled.

I searched the horizon again for my mother's red coat. Maybe the giant bird had picked her up and carried her away, or she'd been injured in the rush to escape. Was she with the ones that got away? My heart grew heavy and my head ached. It had been a whole night and another day. All hope for our reunion vanished as the sun began to sink into the evening sky.

Around me, exhausted horses folded their legs beneath them and lowered their dust-caked bodies to the ground. Parched, they had not yet discovered what the strange container at the far end of the enclosure was for. We saw the water shimmering there, but dared not approach. And as if that weren't bad enough, a gnawing hunger made us restless, but the strange clumps of hay lying on the ground looked like nothing we'd ever nibbled at before. So food, too, went untouched. Bellies empty or full, this was all we had, our life in the wild gone for good.

As the night wore on, I was overcome by sadness. I'd never felt so numb. I sought solace from Tecumseh and dared move closer.

The old stallion stood tired but defiant, his long neck stretched high, his muzzle resting on the upper rail of the enclosure. He watched me, then closed his eyes as if to say, "There's nothing I can do." Defeat hung like a noose around his neck. As the sky finally darkened and another night closed in around us, a perfect crescent moon rose above the horizon.

"What will become of us?" I asked, nickering softly.

"We are doomed," he said. "I have escaped capture all these years, and now—my legs have failed me. I can only tell you this: separation from the wild has come before, and will surely come again—until we are no more.

The two-leggeds will select the young and the strong to serve them until their natural end. Some who were taken before us managed to make it back to us again, back to the open range, and I have heard their stories. They endured many hardships."

"Like what?" I asked.

"Some were ridden hard for days at a time, others branded with burning irons. Some spent their days pulling heavy wagons. You must hope for the best, young one. You might be spared the worst because of your special color, gold like the rays of the sun. Or, you might be prized for your wavy mane and coat, so unique among us."

"My mother always told me I was special," I added. *But no matter. What good was that now?* The thought of being taken away gave me a chill. *Give up my herd?*

"Many moons ago," the old stallion continued, finally looking down into my eyes, "my own grandfather, a leader long before my time, told of a two-legged who captured some of our very best. But he was kind. Along with the Lakota people far to the north who lived off the land and prized

us very much, and who once wove eagle feathers in our manes, this man took these fine horses across the Great Water to be admired by the leaders of many lands. He had long, wavy white hair. It is said he was loved by the horses that served him, and all those who knew him as well. And with your long curly locks, you carry his Indian name—"Pahaska." Longhair. Others called him "Buffalo Bill." Wherever you are headed little one, may you be so lucky to find one who cares for you as he did for the horses he so admired. If you cannot be free, then that is my hope and only wish."

I listened, fascinated by his story, learning so much about my past, but unable to imagine my future or my fate. Would they take me and leave our beloved leader and other band members behind? I paced the fence up and down, dreading the dawn. I didn't want to lose them too.

CHAPTER THREE

To Own a Horse

Jesse Nolan could hardly contain her excitement as she counted off the highway exits enroute to the Rock Springs Wild Horse Holding Facility near Rock Springs, Wyoming. She and her Uncle Joe still had a couple of miles to go and she promised herself she'd stop pestering him with questions, but five minutes at a time was the very best she could do.

"Why do they have to be rounded up at all?" she began, her blue eyes probing Joe's very dark brown ones. He had the same deep-set, brown eyes as her father's, but lighter hair. Side-by-side, no one would ever question they were brothers. In fact, the Nolan brothers were well known and liked in southern Wyoming where they were raised—both working cowboys at one time. Some folks who knew them could hardly tell them apart.

Jesse had inherited her uncle's reddish-blond hair from somewhere in the family's Irish past. Maybe the family temper too. Some in Sweetwater County who didn't know Joe too well actually thought Jesse was his daughter. She often wished she were.

"Well, why don't people just leave the horses where they are?" Jesse continued, adjusting her sunglasses and searching the arid landscape for wildlife. She thought she saw some antelope scatter through the brush.

"Are we back to that again?" Uncle Joe answered, looking at his watch. He slowed for a turn in the road. The well-worn horse trailer, securely hitched behind his Dodge truck, rattled noisily.

"Yes, we are," Jesse answered. "I wish the wild herds could just roam the hills like they always have and go wherever they want to without us bothering them. It doesn't seem fair."

"But you still want to own one, right? Or should we forget the whole thing and turn around?" Uncle Joe flashed a smile, letting her know he was only half-serious.

Jesse didn't answer. She felt her face grow hot as she squelched her reply. Of course she still wanted one! That's all she'd been able to think about for days—for years, maybe. Her very own mustang. *Besides, once the horses were captured, they needed a good home, didn't they?* That thought helped her stay calm.

"I thought we went over everything before we left," Joe said. "Like I told you, wildlife has to be managed. That includes horses. And part of the problem out here is the division of land. The West is all about ranching and borders. That alone makes for some real trouble, and that's just for starters. Not everybody thinks these horses are welcome. Some think they're in the way. It's about sharing resources, something I'm sure you understand. Why don't you think about something else for a while and we can talk more about it later on?"

∞

Uncle Joe never wasted words, but Jesse still had lots of questions. It's partly what drove her to apply for the summer teen internship at the BLM's Southwestern Wyoming Rock Springs Field Office for the second summer in a row. At thirteen, she was the youngest "employee" there. But she was paid a minimum wage by her uncle and worked twenty hours a week. Having a family member on staff helped her get the position, something about "pulling a few strings," Joe said.

For a summer job, it was the best! Uncle Joe arranged for her to work in the very same office where he worked, a bureau that addressed all kinds of issues around Wyoming's wildlife, outdoor recreation, livestock grazing, and of course, wild horses. Most of the time, she was either outdoors with him on some fieldwork assignment, or traveling to a meeting in his truck, and certainly on the road more than she was ever inside at a desk. When in the office, however, she organized files, answered the phone in her most mature voice, and sat in on select committee meetings, taking minutes on her laptop. For a teenager, she was an ace on the keyboard and could type as fast as any secretary. It was all excellent exposure if she wanted a future career in agriculture, or so Uncle Joe said.

Fat chance of that. That's thinking way too far ahead. But Mom said it would look good on a college application someday, so why not?

෴

Jesse loved living with her Aunt Bev and Uncle Joe during the summer. Ever since Mom and Dad split up two years earlier, life at home in Evergreen, Colorado, hadn't been the same. The tension between her parents made her edgy, even though her dad wasn't around all that much. Thank goodness. When he was, they argued over almost anything, adding tinder to a fire that seemed ready to turn into a scorcher. Moving to Wyoming in the summer to be with her favorite uncle for a spell gave her the perfect way out.

Too young to drive a car or have a driver's license, Jesse was often stuck at home during the school year while her mom worked until 5:30 in a nearby bank. If she wanted to go somewhere, she either walked or rode her bike. Most of the time, she went over to her friend Emma Lee's house, just a quarter-mile down Pine Tree Lane.

Emma, always ready to listen, was her VBF, in fact, her very best friend *in the world*. Her mom was American and her father Korean, which Jesse thought was pretty cool. Emma liked *kimchee*, could eat with chopsticks, and could speak two languages. But more than that, she and Jesse both liked techno-pop music, animated *and* action movies, and the same toppings on pizza—pineapple and pepperoni! And their school lockers were actually side-by-side. Jesse was a frequent guest at the Lee house and dinner table. (Emma's mom actually liked to cook.) Sometimes Jesse spent the night, and of course, Emma was just as welcome at her house—well, on weekends anyway.

This past semester, Jesse jumped at the chance to volunteer a few days a week at a small horse boarding facility in her community, "Horse Haven," five easy minutes by bike from the house. Her friends could hardly believe it, but she actually enjoyed cleaning stalls and helping exercise the horses—other people's horses. Just inhaling their scent and being around them made her heady, feeling happy and fulfilled. Somehow, when she was there, she totally lost track of time.

Walking up and down the barn aisle, Jesse memorized every horse's name and what kind of feed they ate, which saddle was theirs in the tack room, and what treats their humans gave them—everything. *One day,* she dared imagine, *I might have a horse too, a horse to brush and blanket, to bridle and saddle, to talk to and to love. And of course, to ride—that would be amazing. That would be worth everything. A horse of my very own.*

༄

The summer flew by. Some days Uncle Joe took Jesse with him on his rounds, meeting with county offices and ranchers. Other times, they'd drive into Granger, a small town in southwestern Wyoming and have lunch at the local Burger King. For fun, Uncle Joe, Aunt Bev and Jesse would all go to the rodeo on Friday nights where they could watch ranch cowboys ride bucking broncs and rope cattle. It was a real tourist attraction. Afterwards there was always a big dance with a loud band and lots of local girls wearing tons of makeup and tight jeans, but Uncle Joe and Aunt Bev never stayed for that part.

"Come on, Jesse," Uncle Joe would say, taking her hand and pushing past all the young cowboys looking her way. "It's time for us to leave."

ം

Fall and a fresh, new school year were fast approaching and Jesse looked forward to seeing her friends again and heading home to Colorado. Eighth grade meant a new curriculum, a new building, a new locker —the works. *Just a few more weeks.* Still, all of that excitement was secondary to today's road trip and her mother's unexpected phone call a few days earlier.

After so many previous conversations that ended nowhere, Lynn Nolan and her husband Travis finally gave in after Uncle Joe told them about the special auction. It was the first time the Bureau of Land Management had decided to hold one. Usually, horses were available for adoption to pre-qualified individuals seeking purchase any time of the year. That way, animals came and went as the opportunity arose. This time though, you had to put in an application, and several buyers at once would be invited to look at a select group of horses that urgently needed a forever home. "It's a limited auction, like a three-hour bidding frenzy," Uncle Joe said.

Whatever, it sounded good to Jesse.

"So look," said Jesse's mom when she called, "if you find a mustang you really want to own, and Uncle Joe approves, and he thinks it's healthy and the right kind of horse for you, then he has our permission to bid on it. You've worked hard all summer. No more than $500 dollars though, that's the limit. Then Uncle Joe will have to arrange for it to be properly gentled before bringing it down to Evergreen. And *then*, young lady…" her mother's voice got deeper, "it will be your responsibility to care for it, as well as get some kind of job to pay for its upkeep from here on out. Is that clear?"

Giving Jesse something to hold onto during the family's turmoil seemed like a good idea to Jesse's mother. Something her daughter could focus on and work hard to nurture.

Had Jesse heard right? Did her mother just offer a deal? *Was she really getting a horse?*

"For real, Mom? My very own horse to care for at last? Are you serious? Oh yes, it's super clear!" Jesse replied. "You bet! And thank you. Thanks so much!"

"You can thank your father, too." Lynn replied. "He's involved here as well. Please don't forget that."

Jesse didn't answer.

∽

Jesse woke up the morning of the auction, climbed into her jeans and favorite red Ropers, and threw on her denim jean jacket. She looked into the mirror as she straightened her hat and pulled up the slide on the hat strings. Her blue eyes blinked back at her under her thick, strawberry blonde brows, and her suntanned cheeks hid a sprinkling of freckles that only bloomed in summer.

She hated those freckles, but not so much today. Because the happiness she felt inside made the corners of her mouth turn up into an irrepressible smile. She grinned and combed her bangs. Today was the day! Unbelievable! She tucked a few stray wisps of hair behind her ears and headed downstairs.

"Don't forget about eating some breakfast," said Aunt Bev. "I made a burrito for you. Your uncle will be along any minute. Good luck today, sweetheart. I hope you find what you're looking for."

"Thanks, Aunt Bev," said Jesse, giving her a hug. She pulled out a chair and sat down, staring at the clock, counting the minutes until she heard Uncle Joe's truck. The burrito disappeared along with a glass of juice. At 8:15, the Dodge engine rumbled to a halt just outside the kitchen door. Joe was back from his morning chores.

"Ready to go, cowgirl?" he said with a wink. "Climb in!"

Cowgirl! He'd never called her that before.

Finally!

Jesse leaned back in the seat and closed her eyes. What kind of horse would they find—if they did? Oh, they just had to, there were so many to choose from. Her special horse *had* to be there. Uncle Joe said the Salt Wells herd came from all different kinds of breeds—American Quarter Horse, Thoroughbred, Arabian, even smaller draft breeds like the Percheron.

Some animals came out of old Native American stock, from horses the Indians had stolen from the settlers long, long ago, and some of those herds descended from the great horses the Spanish conquerors brought to the New World way, way before that, in the 1500s. That was forever ago.

Besides, Jesse wasn't worried. She knew that Joe Nolan could spot a good horse when he saw one. She could trust him there. He'd know what to do. She could trust him with anything.

Uncle Joe was like a good friend who never lost his temper and knew something about everything, especially animals. He'd been married to Aunt Bev for more than twenty years and they were always in a good mood. Even when they didn't agree, they worked things out. Not like her dad and mom who argued about everything. Not like her dad—who left.

Jesse closed her eyes as the wheels of the Dodge covered the ground. *What color and size will my horse be?* she mused. *What will I call it? Will it like me right away? Will it be scared? Never mind. I'll know it when I see it. And no matter where I go, that horse will go with me every step of the way, forever and always, as long as she's happy. She won't mind not being a wild horse anymore. Will she?*

Whoa! Did I say she? But of course. It has to be a filly or a mare—I can hardly wait. My dream is finally coming true.

CHAPTER FOUR

Adoption

"Like I told you at the office, Jesse, they have to split up the herds and remove some animals every year. The Bureau of Land Management likes to keep the numbers low," Uncle Joe explained, as he downshifted and turned into the holding facility entrance. "We need to remove somewhere between 150 to 200 horses each time. I know that doesn't seem like a lot when the range they occupy is almost two million acres over all, but part of that is public land, and that's a problem. A very small amount of that space belongs to the state, and the rest is private. Allowing open range for the wild ones gets complicated."

"Oh, why can't they just leave them alone?" asked Jesse again, ever more their protector.

"Well, they're not out there on their own, you know," he continued. "They're sharing grazing land in some areas. We keep a pretty close watch. Herd growth is monitored by several associations, local and national. Basically, we're trying to curb reproduction and that takes planning, what the office likes to call "sustainability.""

"Whatever that means," said Jesse. *Why does Uncle Joe always have to talk like he's at work?* She guessed it meant whatever was best for everybody. Human beings, that is. *Did anybody ever ask the horses?*

Jesse glanced down at the information page in the pamphlet her uncle gave her, hoping to learn more. One paragraph caught her eye.

"The Rock Springs Wild Horse Holding Facility is the only Federal short-term holding and preparation facility in all of Wyoming, housing approximately 700 wild horses. These are gathered from a variety of herd management areas. The facility also serves as a rest stop for wild horses headed eastbound from other Western states."

A rest stop? She looked at Uncle Joe, her face a question mark. That made it sound like a vacation resort for horses taken off the range. Except she knew it wasn't. For many, this was the last stop before the end. She'd heard that not all the horses got adopted and as they got older, their chances grew less and less. Eventually—she hated to think about it. Some ended up in a slaughterhouse, over the borders in Mexico and Canada. No one wanted to talk about that. But it was also part of the story. The dark side.

Uncle Joe told her you never knew what you'd see at the auction, or who, since the animals and buyers varied so much. Folks came from all over. Horses as well. Viewers were welcome year-round, but the combined auctions, created to sell more animals, were only held twice a year in March and August. Good thing her parents got together with Uncle Joe on this one. She sure was lucky; the timing was perfect.

༄

Joe entered the parking area and began circling the lot, searching for a place to park the truck and trailer. Finding a secure spot, they got out, and headed up onto the viewing platform, high enough over the herd to see the horses clearly.

The animals bunched out on the few acres of land where they'd been gathered. Most just stood with their heads down. They seemed listless and bored, indifferent, in fact. But the view was dizzying. Some six hundred horses filled the enclosure. It was hard to imagine these animals running free and playing in their family bands. Surrounded by a high fence, they looked sad, nothing like the wild horses Jesse had seen in films or pictures, or that she had so often dreamed about.

"Today," said Joe, "about a third of these will be selected, most between two to eight years old. We've got bays, paints, sorrels, and chestnuts, plus horses with gray coats, spotted coats, even coal black, to choose from. You can take your pick from the string they bring out later. Hopefully we'll find a young one if possible."

To Jesse, each one was more beautiful than the next. Some had snips on their noses; others had blazes, stars, or other unusual markings that set them apart. One thing was for sure—they all begged to be free. You could feel it in the way they looked at you, with deep, somber eyes.

Some horses had coats like speckled silver, but one in particular shone almost like gold. She stood far off in a corner of the enclosure near a handsome bay, a small yellow-colored filly. Some might have said she was a palomino, but Jesse couldn't be too sure. She had a full, blonde, curly coat and a creamy, wavy mane. She looked young, maybe not more than two or three years old, but had strong legs and a beautiful neck and head.

Oh, I hope she's in the auction today, thought Jesse. She craned her neck to see better, sizing her up from nose to tail. The curly-coated filly turned when she felt Jesse's gaze upon her. Her spiral forelock fell between her ears, framing an elegant, expressive face with big brown eyes rimmed by long lashes. Her fuzzy ears pricked in Jesse's direction as if to say, "Who are you?"

"Oh look Uncle Joe, she sees me!" Jesse's heart began to pound. "She's looking right at me! It's as if she knows me already. Oh, she's so pretty. She's the one I want. That little golden filly is the perfect horse for me!"

CHAPTER FIVE

Be Careful What You Wish For

"Don't resist," said the bay horse standing next to little Pahaska. "It looks like they're coming for us. We've been chosen. Just follow me and then go wherever they ask you to go, no matter what. If you see a chute or an opening and it means you have to go that way, do it. Trust me. I've been through this before."

Pahaska didn't know what to think when the man on horseback starting waving something long and snaky at them. She followed the bay horse and all the others who were trying to get away. In a minute however, they were lined up, single file, along the edge of the enclosure, headed to the auction corral. There, they'd be let out one-by-one to pass through a smaller pen in front of the bidders, for better or worse.

Pahaska began to sweat, turning her cream-colored chest a damp shade of brown. *Please don't hurt me*, she worried. Being separated from the herd frightened her, and the hiss of the rope slicing through the air made her tremble in fear.

Just over two hundred horses were to be presented that day. After the bidding, those that got sold would be sorted into loading pens fitted with ramps for stock trailers. Some horses were lucky enough to be purchased by individual horse owners; others might be headed to cattle ranches to be used in a *remuda,* or sold to roughstock handlers to be used for the rodeo. Trailer loading proved to be the next hurdle for many, both a frightening, and sometimes even a deadly experience.

What should I do now? Pahaska wondered as she felt herself pushed forward into the dusty corral. A metal gate slammed behind her. Off to one side, customers sitting on bleachers snapped photos with cell phones and took notes. The little golden filly's entrance provoked a round of "ooohs" and "aaahs" from the buyers.

I think I'm going to faint! she thought, shaking from nose to tail. Pahaska began trotting in circles and tossing her head. Her legs felt like they would buckle and then—they did. Her knees went down first, and then her neck and head dropped to the ground.

Buyers in the bleachers thought she just wanted to roll, and laughed out loud when she went down. Some people cheered.

Pahaska groaned. She rolled flat to one side, laying her head in the dust, hoping that if she just closed her eyes, all this would somehow disappear.

"Get up, Blondie," the auctioneer called over the microphone. "Come on now—show us what you're made of! Who'll give me a hundred dollars for this fine young filly? A hundred once. A hundred twice…"

The auctioneer started to work the buyers and Pahaska clambered to her feet. She shook off the dust and hung her head, eyeing the crowd. The strange smell of so many humans confused her. What did they want? Why wouldn't they leave her alone?

Within minutes the offers started to climb, first to two hundred, then to three-seventy-five, then to four hundred dollars. Then to four hundred and twenty-five—going once, twice.

"Do I hear fifty? Four hundred and fifty? Do I hear five? Five hundred once? Five hundred?"

Uncle Joe raised his paddle and called out four hundred and seventy-five dollars, top price, take it or leave it. Jesse stood up too, unable to sit any longer, her face flushed with excitement. She held her breath.

"Going once. Going twice. Sold to the man from the BLM and the pretty little lady sitting by his side! You're one lucky girl, Miss Nolan," he said. "Owner of a fine, three-year-old Curly. Yes, ma'am, you got yourself a good horse there. Yes indeed! Next up—who'll give me fifty for the bay?"

CHAPTER SIX

A Tough Surprise

At first Jesse couldn't even speak. Then she stood on the toes of her boots and grabbed Uncle Joe's shoulders and almost jumped into his arms, ecstatic with joy. "Oh thank you!" she gushed, taking a deep breath, tears misting in her eyes. "Thanks, Uncle Joe—I can't believe it! My own wild Curly. And a filly too. My beautiful Curly Girl!"

They headed down to the payment desk and while Uncle Joe arranged all the details and filled out the necessary papers, Jesse went to grab a soda from the concession. As planned, her uncle would take the golden filly down to his ranch for a few weeks of gentling, and introduce her to a halter, lead rope and saddle; all the things he was sure Jesse couldn't do on her own. Not with a wild one. Then he'd bring the horse to Colorado to start her new life.

Although Jesse would be heading back home to begin school in a few days, at least the filly and her new human would get to spend some time together before she left, enough to get acquainted and make friends. So many changes, new people, and new experiences! Jesse couldn't even imagine how her Curly Girl would react. But if anyone could transform something wild into something tame, Jesse was sure Uncle Joe could do it with ease.

A few of the sold animals had been turned out in a corral behind the auction pen where they waited for buyers to claim them.

"Could I go down and be with her please?" Jesse asked, taking a long drink from her soda.

"No, I think you'd better stay here with me. Why don't you make sure we have fresh water in the trailer meanwhile, and hay in the rack. I wouldn't want you to get hurt down there. After all, those horses in the pen are still a bit riled up."

Jesse went to the trailer and readied the water pail and feed net. Then she leaned against the trailer and waited, counting the minutes. Why was the line so long? Paperwork was *so* time-consuming. By the time Joe flagged her to join him and walk down to the pens, most of the horses had already been loaded and taken away. Anxious, Jesse went from one enclosure to the next, but Curly Girl was nowhere to be found.

"Uncle Joe, something's wrong," said Jesse. She climbed up the fence rail to get a better look. "She's not here. Only three horses left and she's not one of them."

Just as she spoke, she noticed a long, dilapidated stock trailer slowly exiting the parking lot. It had Texas license plates. Between the slats glimmered a golden coat. Horses bound for slaughter went to Mexico through Texas, horses no one wanted. That couldn't be her, could it? Her little horse couldn't be in that awful place. But Uncle Joe saw it too. "Well, look at that! I'll be darned!" he said. "It looks like she's in that trailer!"

The tears that only misted in Jesse's eyes after securing Curly Girl at the auction now coursed freely down her cheeks. "Oh no! It can't be! Hurry, Uncle Joe! We have to catch them! Please, please, don't let them get away!"

Joe Nolan took out his cell phone and tapped in 911. "Yes ma'am, Nolan here, BLM. Need some back-up please, we've got a horse thief on the run. We're talking a twenty-foot stock trailer with roughly a dozen animals heading toward Interstate 80. We're giving chase. I'm driving a blue pickup, white horse trailer attached. He's got a quarter-mile head start at least. Use aerial support if you have to. We've got personal merchandise on that rig, bought and paid for."

Jesse couldn't keep the tears from falling as she thought of her wild filly stolen by some awful stranger. She looked out the window as they sped out of the parking lot and prayed they'd catch the thief. Meanwhile, she didn't want Uncle Joe to see her cry. But she couldn't help it. Her dream had been shattered. How dare someone snatch her horse right out from under her!

To Jesse, Curly was the prize of the lot, the prettiest horse in the auction. Guess somebody else thought so too. She might bring even more money south of the border, or just her curly golden hide. No telling what they might use her for. What an awful thought!

"Step on the gas, Uncle Joe, please!"

∞

Curly Girl struggled in the heat. She stood next to Tecumseh who had also been taken, both animals packed in so tight they could barely breathe. The vehicle was an old stock trailer, with floor to ceiling metal slats, like a giant box. Loaded sideways, head to tail, the horses might be headed for a long and difficult journey across Wyoming, Utah, and down through Arizona and Texas, until they crossed the Mexican border. No food, no water, nothing but nine hundred miles of highway, dust and fumes. Many would never survive the journey.

Curly was nearest the tailgate so she managed to get slightly more air, but nothing in her short, young life had prepared her for this.

"Where are we going?" she whinnied.

"I don't know," answered Tecumseh. "I'm not sure. And I'm not sure I want to know. Try to stay on your feet little one, or you'll be trampled. Go ahead, lean on me."

Curly Girl peered out between the slats on her side, near the tailgate, watching the landscape speed by. In the distance, nearly a half-mile behind them, a blue Dodge truck with a trailer behind was slowly gaining distance. But she couldn't process that.

Curly closed her brown eyes and shuddered all the way down to her neat, small hooves, now buried in several inches of muck. All she could think of was freedom—the grassy hills she used to climb, her mother's warm flank, the night breeze in the sky—even the soft feel of wind in her mane. She remembered the heat of the late summer sun on her back only days before, and the cool, crisp nights of early fall, thinking back to the first kiss of winter snowflakes falling on her nose.

Where was any of that now? Blinking hard, all she could comprehend this minute was that her entire world had disintegrated into the filthy, manure-filled confines of a horse hauler's truck.

CHAPTER SEVEN

Rescue

A pair of Wyoming state troopers in a patrol car zoomed by and moved ahead of the big trailer, forcing the driver to slow down. "Pull over!" they barked through a microphone. They drove on ahead, parked their car, and approached the massive carrier as it came to a stop by the side of the road. The two officers stood beneath the driver's door.

"Get out of the vehicle, gentlemen," they ordered.

The driver, a man with a broad-rimmed cowboy hat, pretended not to understand. His partner, visibly shaken, began to fumble through the truck glove compartment.

"License, please. And step down, now! *Pronto!*"

The driver finally complied, opening the door and climbing down to the roadside, groping for his wallet.

Looking at the driver's license, notably issued in Texas, the closest officer asked, "You have proof of purchase for these animals?"

The driver seemed not to comprehend, shrugging his shoulders and shaking his head.

But his partner nodded, affirming that they did.

"Ok, let's cut to the chase," the other officer said. "We think you have stolen property on board. *Documents now!*"

The driver's partner reached for his back pocket, and began to unfold what looked like an auction bill of sale. At the very same time, Jesse and Joe pulled up behind, parked the Dodge, and got out.

"You stole my horse!" shouted Jesse, approaching the driver, her eyes red, brimming with tears. "How dare you!"

The driver didn't answer.

Uncle Joe showed the officers his purchase papers, describing Curly Girl in detail, her blonde-colored coat, freeze brand, (which had been applied the morning after her arrival), markings and size.

"Sure looks like her," said one officer to the other, peering into the big stock trailer through the slats. "Yeah, I'd say that's her alright."

Uncle Joe confirmed her claim, took out his wallet and driver's license, and identified himself as the one who just purchased the animal.

Scanning the truck driver's bill of sale, the first officer could see clearly there was no blonde filly listed. "OK. No further discussion." Turning to the driver once more, the trooper said, "Now open the trailer, sir."

"No, no. That's not possible," the driver protested. Then the officer pulled out a pair of handcuffs. Suddenly the man understood. The man's eyes widened in fear.

"You heard what I said, Buster. Unlatch that tailgate. Now!"

The driver reluctantly obliged, heading to the back of the trailer. "It's a mistake," he said. "No problem. Totally a big mistake."

"It looks like we need to book you two for theft, sir," said the first trooper. "We'll need to go over your documents, one animal at a time," said the other. "You're under arrest. You'll have to return this rig to Rock Springs until we get to the bottom of this. We'll escort you all the way. Who do you work for anyway?"

As the officers wrote up the citation and explained what would happen next, Uncle Joe shook out a loop on his rope, preparing to drop it over the filly's head when the tailgate opened. Luckily the wide gate would serve as a ramp so she wouldn't have to jump down. That would make it easier to grab her, and after all, Joe had been a great roper in his day.

As the big metal back gate fell forward to the ground, the horses inside began to rear and stomp. The rush of air excited all of them. Curly, closest to the door, pushed against a heavy metal chain.

"Please," the driver begged. "Take only this one horse." Suddenly the chain snapped open as the pressure of many animals surged forward. The horses had started to push. Desperate whinnies and cries filled the air. Tecumseh nudged Curly from behind. "Go quickly, little one. Down! Now!"

But before Curly could take two steps, a loop settled neatly over her neck and pulled tight, catching her under the throat.

Aaack! she choked. She jumped to the ground off the ramp and skittered off to one side, turning a half circle, held fast by Joe's taut, firm rope. *What to do now? This hurts!!*

The truck driver meanwhile waved a whip at the other animals that were starting to move toward the opening, attempting to push them back. Curly Girl continued to prance at the end of Joe's rope, desperate to free herself.

"Come on girl, you're OK. Settle down." The man's voice was kind. She looked at him with one ear cocked forward. *What did he want?*

"Come on now. Easy." He pulled her toward a white trailer behind his truck, its tailgate opened wide. To her, the inside looked like a cave. But within was a manger filled with grass hay next to a bucket of water. It smelled good and she was hungry. To either side of the hay rack, small windows offered plenty of light.

"Come on girl, you're heading home."

Home? Home?

Before Curly could ponder what that meant, a huge semi came barreling down the road behind them. Its engine's roar frightened her and she jumped straight into the trailer, the only safe place she could see.

At that very moment, Tecumseh, determined not to stay in the suffocating hauler's trailer one more second, leapt as far and fast as his

old legs could carry him—a leap that carried him high above the men below on the ground, down the ramp and out! Hooves flying, he hit the side of the road, throwing dirt and gravel into the air. As he touched the earth beneath his feet, the once proud stallion of the Salt Wells band galloped across the ground toward the far-away hills. Neck stretched long, nose into the wind, he thundered off, determined to never, ever be caught again.

"Run!" called Curly Girl from inside her new berth, watching his white tail fade into the distance. Her high pitched whinny soared across the prairie. "Run, Tecumseh, run!"

CHAPTER EIGHT

Home on the Ranch

Was this what they called home? Curly Girl wondered. They'd come to a stop after many miles on the road. She looked through the side windows before backing out of the trailer. This didn't look anything like the home she'd come from. What kind of place was it?

Before her stood a building flanked by corrals and an enclosure where an animal she didn't recognize at all stood nibbling on some hay. She followed the man with the kind voice toward the arena—that's what he called it. He opened the gate, loosened the rope, and let her free. Then, the smaller two-legged with the blonde hair (a girl, she learned it was called) approached and stood behind the enclosure to watch.

Curly took a few steps and stopped to study the small creature a few feet away. It had very long ears and looked like a horse, except for those ears.

The animal met her gaze. Curly stood, not moving a muscle, waiting for something to happen. Anything. Suddenly a strange, loud, almost deafening noise erupted from the animal, a kind of whinny, like nothing she'd ever heard before, asking "Who are you?"

"I am Pahaska! Or maybe, Curly Girl. That's what the human called me before I left in that big thing that rolls. She said it over and over again, so I guess that must be my new name."

"Welcome, Curly Girl," said Big Ears. "I am Chaco."

Curly trotted over to say hi. Out of nowhere appeared a small, bright colored, four-footed ferret—no, maybe it was a bobcat or a weasel. It jumped up on Chaco's back and sat, staring with round, yellow eyes and small triangular ears. *How could that happen?*

Chaco let it stay, not shaking it off. This was a strange place indeed.

"Not to worry," said Chaco. "That's just my good friend, Buddy. He's a cat."

"A cat," Curly repeated. She filed the word away for the next time. Home certainly had some unusual residents. "Nice to meet you. I don't mean to be rude, but you talk funny for a horse."

"That's because I'm not a horse. Nope. I'm a burro," he said. "Similar, but different. Get used to it."

What happens next? worried Curly Girl. *What should I do?*

The humans left her on her own to get settled but she couldn't. Everything seemed so different, so new. After a few more words with Chaco, she headed off to explore the enclosure.

She paced. She rolled in the dust and trotted round and round. *Where was the stream? The herd? Fresh grass to pull? This can't be home! There's dead grass on the ground and water in a big container, but nothing feels right. Chaco said I'm just homesick and it would pass. He said he came from far away once too, and was adopted by the man and his mate. Back then they had an old horse that needed a friend, but that horse went away one day and never came back.*

"Don't worry," Chaco assured her. "It gets better. You'll like the human with the yellow hair especially. She's real nice. We're all glad you're here. Little Buddy and I get lonely sometimes."

∽

Later that day, the man and the girl came to my pen. She called my name and reached out her hand. I wasn't sure about anything just then, so I stayed where I was.

"Don't be afraid, Curly," the girl said. "You'll get to know me soon enough. And you'll be home before you know it. See you soon. I'll be waiting for you."

Home? Wait a minute. There's that word again. Home. What did she mean? I thought this was home. I thought that's what they said.

The man came into my pen. I stood my ground and let him approach. He got very close to me and reached for my neck. Then I bolted. Whew! No one on two legs had ever been that near before. A close call.

He tried again. I sniffed and trembled where I stood, four hooves planted on the ground. He got closer, and this time, I stood still, snorting away my fear. He talked real low and ran his hand down my back, what I later learned was called my withers. I shivered. It felt good. I was so surprised. He started to walk, real slow, around the pen, talking to me all the while, and I decided to follow him. Maybe he'd touch me again. The whole time the girl watched from behind the fence. Sometimes she held something small and black to her eye and I could hear it go click, click, click.

Over time, the man and I became friends. He rubbed and scratched my neck as I stood quietly. His touch was better than the best tree I'd ever rubbed against. I didn't even mind when he slipped something around my neck and let it hang there for a while. (He told me it was called a rope and not to be afraid.) I tried to shake it off but it stayed. No matter. It didn't scare me. Eventually, he put more of it around my face, on and off, over and over. He said it was a halter, something I'd need later on, and that it looked pretty on me. When we were done one afternoon, I followed him to the gate and watched him walk back into the house. I hung my head over the fence. I hoped he'd come again.

∞

The next morning the man came into my corral. This time the girl came with him. I let her approach me and touch my neck. I smelled her hand, but that was all. One two-legged at a time. The girl stood near me and waited. I watched her, not sure what she wanted.

Finally she said, "I have to go away soon and I came to say goodbye, Curly Girl. I have to go back to Colorado. Be good and learn everything Uncle Joe has to teach you. I'll see you before you know it! Don't forget me."

Time passed and I learned a lot more about what it means to belong to someone. I got used to eating the dried grass that had been cut and left for me to chew, and how to drink out of something called a tank. Although one day, I discovered the trickle of snowmelt from the barn roof coming through a pipe, fresh and sweet. It reminded me of the spring runoff when snows used to melt on the rocks. *That's more like it*, I said to myself, enjoying the treat.

I learned all about wearing the halter, being led by a rope, and tolerating something on my back called a blanket. Off and on, over and over, until I forgot it was there. Training was fun. It gave me something to do besides stand around and mope. But when I was alone, when I had nothing but long hours and time to myself, I couldn't help but think about my life before this and how it felt to be free, and my mother and old Tecumseh, and all the others too. Did our leader find another band to run with? Did he get caught by humans again?

Most of all, I thought a lot about a special honor awarded to me by my band the season before our capture. It was my grandest adventure, my proudest achievement. My mother told me afterward that I had earned the entire herd's respect, and that what I did back then would make me into a fine lead mare one day, a very important rank for a wild horse.

One night I started to tell Chaco about the life I led when I was free.

"Go on," he said. "Tell me everything!" He wanted the whole story.

"Well," I began, "it was during the time when the snow falls and we all needed to be together to stay warm. Somehow, some of our band went missing. Thanks to me though, they were saved."

I didn't want to sound like I was bragging, but that's the honest truth.

"Saved? What happened, exactly?" he asked. "I want to hear all about it."

"OK," I said, thinking back to the time before we were captured. "It went like this…"

CHAPTER NINE

Becoming a Warrior

"Among the older horses in our band, the one I never understood was Rocky, a four-year-old grulla. That's a special color, a deep shade of grayish-blue. It seems like horses this color are tough and independent, or so I was told. Rocky however, was also scrappy and ill-mannered, and often in trouble with Pawnee, our respected lead mare. Someday, we all knew he would head out on his own as most bachelor stallions do and form his own herd, but until then, he tested everyone's patience, including mine.

I was not much more than a yearling, maybe eighteen months old. But I was a good listener and a good observer too. I tried to mind my manners and learn everything my mother taught me. Sticking together was, and is, the first rule. Horses that get separated risk everything—exposure to hunters, mountain lions, weather—everything.

Rocky didn't care about any of that. He made his own rules, for better or worse. One brisk November day, he and two of his buddies, Oho and Red, took off and high-tailed it to a ridge far above our grazing area. From there, they galloped across the hills and over and down, descending into a steep canyon. It had several ravines that looked like ways to get out, but weren't. The only route out was the way in, and it was much harder to climb up than slide down, which is what they did on the descent. Besides, the entry was a narrow passage from above and extremely hard to see from below.

That day the temperature dropped. We all knew winter was on its way. Our coats had grown thick and deep, and the green Wyoming grass had long turned brown. A serious winter blizzard was just a matter of time. By mid-afternoon, we all saw dense clouds billowing on the horizon. The horses gathered in a circle, tails to the wind, preparing for the worst. But Rocky, Oho and Red were nowhere to be found.

Pawnee, our lead mare, began to circle and whinny, searching the places she knew best for any sign of them. A good lead mare always knows where her band roams. She called, over and over, her frantic neighs filling the air. Using her strong sense of smell, she galloped through the lower valley and searched the ravines, retracing the territory we frequented for many miles. Finally she trotted back to our cluster. Night had begun to fall, dark shadows filling the hollows. Something was very wrong. Pawnee lifted her head to the wind and closed her eyes, trying to capture their scent. Nothing—nothing but the smell of snow, as sure as she could feel the wind in her nostrils. Winter had arrived. She must find the young, lost horses somehow and protect the group. But how?

I was as worried as everyone. We'd never lost members of our band before. Tecumseh paced and thundered about, furious that they had disobeyed the foremost rule of survival—togetherness. They'd have to pay. But meanwhile, he couldn't abandon his herd and search for them. His place was here, as guardian, a lookout for danger. They would have to come back on their own.

A cold night passed and the first snowfall left its cover upon the ground. For some of us, its fluffy whiteness was novel and fun. But Rocky's mother, still nursing a young filly born a season late, was beside herself; so distraught in fact, she wouldn't let her baby nurse. It followed her desperately, nudging and asking, but she just kept moving, pacing, circling the band, wondering where her son had gone.

That was it! Someone had to find them. I wasn't sure I'd be successful, but I remembered seeing them, more than once, heading up and over the ridge. Maybe I could still catch their scent if I went the same way.

It was morning and the wind had blown off the light dusting of snow. I could see tracks, hoof prints in the earth below, and followed them

until I reached an overlook, beyond any distance we had ever gone. I hesitated. Far below me lay a canyon with a creek running through its heart.

I bet they're down there, I said to myself. It was just a hunch, and all I had to go on, but I decided to give it a try. First, I took note of the way I had come, leaving marks here and there, and then headed down, down, and down some more. The going was hard and steep, much more than I imagined, and I slid part of the way on my rump. To make things worse, snow had begun to fall again, much harder this time, making it hard to see. But something felt right. If not, I would have a long climb back up, all for nothing.

Following the creek, I called Rocky by name. My shrill whinny echoed off the canyon walls. I called again and again. This time, a faint neigh came back to me. *Yes! What was that?*

I had an answer. I recognized the sound. It was Oho!

"Where are you?" he called.

"I am here, by the water," I answered. "On the far side of the trees. Come find me."

Within minutes, the trio came splashing through the shallow water, looking much relieved. They had been huddled under a broad-branched pine, cold and shivering, waiting for…what? They flung their heads in recognition and whinnied again.

"What are you doing way out here, Pahaska?" asked Red, too embarrassed to say thanks for coming.

"Looking for you," I answered. "What do you think? Someone had to!" I turned to Rocky. "Shame on you. You've risked everyone's life this way, running off to places you don't know."

Rocky just snorted, kicked up his heels and bared his teeth.

"Now let's get out of here," I said. "It's late."

"But how?" asked Red. "We've been searching for an exit for hours. We've lost the trail."

"Back this way," I answered. "I know how. Follow me."

By then the snow was falling in thick gusts, swirling all around. It made the climb up the canyon much harder than ever, but we picked our way, step by step. When we got to the top, I was thankful I had chomped on some of the trees, using them as markers for the trail, because in the snowstorm, all directions were beginning to look the same. The swirling wind made it hard to see, but slowly we wended our way through the forest and back up on to the high ridge. Somewhere above us, a winter hawk fluttered off of a high branch, showering us with snow. We all looked up and saw the bird soar away, disappearing into the sky. I resumed my lead, and without another word, the three bachelors followed me home.

We arrived back to the herd, now clustered in a protective draw, huddled together for warmth. The snow had stopped falling, and a few horses sought the last rays of the afternoon sun. Snow glistened where the sunlight fell upon it, and long blue shadows lay like purple branches against the whiteness. Pawnee smelled us coming and whinnied her excitement, galloping around the herd, trumpeting our return. Rocky's

mother sighed a huge sigh of relief and let her baby nurse again. We were a wild horse family, at peace once more."

"Then what happened?" asked Chaco, his eyes wide, his long ears erect to catch every single word and swiveling in anticipation. "This is the best story I ever heard! Please, tell me more!"

Buddy, still on Chaco's back, stretched and changed positions, the white tip of his tail wrapped around his nose. He couldn't even imagine such an adventure. The very idea of being lost terrified him. So did snow, anything wet at all.

"Well, then," I answered, "Pawnee decided to make a ceremony in my honor. She arranged for the black crows that often followed our herd, along with some of our mares, to weave raven feathers into my mane. Then Tecumseh decorated my chest with an Indian breastplate he found hanging from a tree once near an abandoned Indian camp. It was so beautiful, carved out of buffalo bone, with hawk bells and beads upon it."

"Wow," said Chaco, wide-eyed.

"This is for a brave warrior," Tecumseh said to me, in front of everyone. My mother and father stood proudly to either side, their heads bowed in respect. He continued. "This is for one who is deemed worthy of being a leader. For Pahaska, the youngest leader of our tribe, a leader of our herd."

As he spoke, the hawk sailed overhead and crowned the occasion by making a wide loop in the sky, like the letter P.

"The hawk did it for me, Chaco! Can you imagine? You should have seen it. It was really something! Rocky said it was just a puffy cloud, but I knew better. You know—I didn't think I deserved all the honors, but the other horses did. That was my proudest day."

"Boy, I'll say!" said Chaco. "Of course you deserved it! Hey, did you hear all that, Buddy, did you?"

Buddy's eyes shown sleepily through golden slits, and his pink tongue swept once slowly over his whiskers. He seemed to say yes. Then he wrapped himself even tighter into a ball, falling asleep on top of Chaco's back.

CHAPTER TEN

Waiting

"I hear your new horse is arriving soon," said Sandy to Jesse, leading her big gray mare out of the stall. Sandy Wiggins owned the Swedish Warmblood at Horse Haven Stables, a hunter-jumper who could leap fences and prance when she walked. Sandy called her "Belle." Belle was a registered showhorse bred in northern Europe somewhere and worth thousands of dollars, or so Sandy said. Belle was only ridden under an English saddle and competed in big shows statewide. Sandy even had her own double horse trailer with a walk-in dressing room.

"Oh yes," I answered, "my horse *is* coming soon," hoping I sounded confident.

To be honest, I had no idea when Curly would come. But at least Sandy was talking to me. That was something. Up until now, I was just the dumb kid who cleaned the stalls. A nobody. Some honor. Besides, I'm not sure I ever liked Sandy Wiggins, not even the slightest bit.

○○○

Emma Lee phoned every afternoon after school wondering if I'd heard anything yet. "Is she here? Is she here?" she would ask over and over.

"No," I answered. "You'd know if she was."

Everyone was so excited. I knew Emma meant well but it was hard to say "I don't know" every single day. It was hard to wait. How could anything take so long?

Each day seemed to drag on forever, in spite of school starting, and in spite of my new job—babysitting three days a week from four until six-thirty taking care of our neighbor's fourth-grade twins. OK, so babysitting isn't too cool, but what else could I find that would almost pay for an entire month's board? Every dollar mattered, and my allowance didn't help much. Mom and Dad said the horse expense was going to be mine. So I arranged to feed Curly Girl myself to get a discount—almost a hundred dollars a month. Even though it meant getting up extra early before school to do so, and going over every afternoon before dinner, I didn't care. I wanted to. I really did.

As promised, I was keeping up with my homework too, for the first time maybe, ever. My grades weren't half bad. In fact, they were pretty good. Somehow, school seemed easier this year. Dad wouldn't have to complain about me slacking off anymore, *if* he were around. And we probably wouldn't be arguing like we used to, either. Anyway, it seemed like I was busy from morning till night, all while I was waiting and waiting, and hoping and hoping. It's weird, but every single day for me revolved around a horse that wasn't there.

༄

As soon as I got back from Wyoming in early September, Mom put down a deposit to hold a stall at Horse Haven, one with a nice run that measured a full 12 feet wide by 20 feet long. I promised to pay her back when I could. I was sure Curly Girl would appreciate the space, the last one in a long row of stalls with a roomy turnout. A horse could see the whole pasture from there; five full acres to the property line. In the spring and summer, every horse would be turned out in that pasture to graze. Horse Heaven if you ask me.

Oh, I just know she's going to love it. She's got to. And it's so close to the house, I can see her whenever I want. Every day. Twice a day. I just need her to come. Soon.

༄

September limped by. Four whole weeks of waiting and hoping, watching Mustang Makeover reruns. That's a competition to gentle wild horses in a specific time frame, done by real horse trainers who are famous, and also by some people who aren't. On top of that, I went to the library and stayed up nights reading everything I could get my hands on about training your own horse. I checked out regular training videos too. It didn't seem that hard. Except they all said wild horses are often unpredictable. But I do know how to ride after all; I've been doing that since I was a kid. Mom made sure I took riding lessons when I was in kindergarten. Plus I went to camp. I guess I've been horse crazy since I was born.

Some nights, I took an old rag and oiled my Western saddle that sat on a stand in the middle of my room. Then I'd sit on it and close my eyes and pretend that Curly and I were riding in the wind, heading over a hill. I cleaned up the leather headstall and reins as well, for the day when they would slip over Curly Girl's pretty head. Just for fun, I read *My Friend Flicka* again, and *Smoky the Cowhorse*, too.

༄

Fall was in full swing with crisp mornings and cool nights, the days growing shorter and shorter, but still no Curly Girl. A fresh page on the calendar would begin the next day with a brand new month—October 1st.

How could that be? Curly Girl's pictures, taken back in Wyoming at Uncle Joe's in August, were already pasted over every new calendar month all the way to March, but Uncle Joe still hadn't given us an arrival date. I'm worried. He hasn't called for days. What could be keeping him? Last time we spoke on the phone, he said everything was going "well enough." Well enough? What did that mean? Mom said to be patient. Joe knows what he's doing.

OK, I said. OK. But I don't think I can stand much more of this. Really, I can't. Soon it will be Thanksgiving. I hope she'll be here by then.

CHAPTER ELEVEN

School Time

"Whoa, little one," said Joe, slacking the rope. "Slow down." He drew in the lunge line and pulled the filly to a trot. Curly Girl had taken to the halter easily enough, and the lead rope with little resistance. In almost four weeks she'd learned to follow nicely, turn right and left, walk up to the gate *and* back away from it, lift her feet, and lunge in the arena on the lunge line at a full gallop. She'd also stand quietly when Joe approached her.

Fair enough.

Friendly and curious, there was just something Joe Nolan couldn't put his finger on. The horse was fearful. Any loud noise reduced her to a quivering mass, pouring sweat, tossing her head. She'd fidget and paw the ground. Crazy! He wondered whatever could have caused such a reaction in a horse this young. Whatever it was, it wasn't good. She might not be safe.

Joe kept trying. He knew he needed Curly Girl's total trust. Treats and kind words came with every lesson. Another week passed. The pad and saddle blanket had been accepted pretty well, laying them on her back and withers until she paid them no mind. Then one morning, he slipped a bosal, a braided rawhide bridle without a bit, over her head and halter, and let that lie too, dropping the reins in a knot up over her neck. She accepted that quietly as well, hanging her head, testing the feel of it.

"Good girl." He straightened her forelock and petted the long bridge of her nose. A bridle and bit would come later.

But the saddle was another story. Not surprisingly, she wouldn't have any of it. First time he laid it on her she almost went through the fence. Second time wasn't much better. Joe tied her up short to a post and left the saddle on the ground, within viewing distance. Curly backed away as far as she could get from it, and snorted and blew for over half an hour.

When he finally got it on her back and cinched it lightly, she started to buck like crazy, cantering around and around the pen until the whole thing began to slip sideways, then all the way around her belly, upside down! But even that didn't stop her. Somehow, she succeeded in bucking the whole thing off until the saddle and the pad slid clear down her haunches and lay on the ground in a heap, etched with her hoof prints on the dusty leather seat.

"Whew! That was close," said Joe. *What a train wreck! She could have broken a leg, or worse. And that was a nice saddle too.* He shook his head. *This might take longer than I thought.*

※

A brief warm spell of Indian summer kept October balmy and comfortable. The lessons continued, each day showing improvement from the last.

A few times a week, Joe rode his own horse and took Curly out alongside, leading her. His Quarter Horse mare, Peanut, was so calm and peaceful—solid as a rock. Joe enjoyed ponying the young filly along the ranch trails so she might learn to be part of the outside world, on *his* terms. Curly Girl seemed to love it, following along like a dog on a leash, ears pricked, catching every sound. Such a cute little thing.

But was she safe enough for his beloved niece? Joe's brother Travis would never forgive him if Jesse got hurt. Even though father and daughter hadn't been getting along too well since the split, Joe knew that Travis adored Jesse and wanted very much to heal the rift. This horse was a peace offering in a way. He wondered if Jesse realized it.

※

Uncle Joe knew the weather wouldn't hold. He needed to get Curly Girl used to loading in a trailer and completely comfortable under saddle, then on to Colorado before the snow fell. He didn't want to be driving in a storm. Much needed to be done before the trip.

Loading her into the horse trailer went surprisingly well. For starters, he backed the trailer up to the arena during the day for an entire week and kept the gate down, but filled the manger full of hay, so the filly could walk in and out of it whenever she wanted and enjoy a treat. She could visit it by choice that way, and she did.

Finally, the calendar told Joe the time had come. Curly Girl needed to get to her real family. The two needed to have some time together before riding outdoors was impossible. But the horse had to be good and ready.

Approaching Curly Girl with his saddle slung under his arm, Joe decided this was the day. "Easy does it," he whispered, as he placed the saddle upon the pad, already on her back. To his surprise, the filly stood still and quiet, and even let him buckle the girth without flinching. Then he placed his foot into the stirrup and mounted up, gently swinging the other leg over her, slow and steady. No reaction at all.

Then he dismounted and stood by her side. "Good girl," he said and gave her a pat. *Well, what do you know?* Another try and she tolerated that too. A third time and he mounted up and simply sat for some minutes, stroking her neck.

"That's a *very* good girl," he said. "Shall we go for a ride?" He settled deeper into the seat, expecting her to buck at any moment.

Finally, she wiggled her ears and turned her head to look back at him as if to say, "What are you doing up there? Let's go!"

Joe patted her on the neck again and smiled. *Maybe she's ready after all.* He urged her forward into the arena where she tested him with a single short buck and a hop, and that was it. She settled down into an easy walk and responded to every squeeze of his calves or touch of his heels as he prompted her around the arena. Remarkable. She was a natural. Joe turned her toward the open gate; why not try the trail?

Curly Girl lowered her head and ambled over the worn path, carrying Joe as if she'd been a trail horse all her life. He marveled at her gentle nature and sharp response, picking her way over branches and stones, carefully maneuvering the trail. He decided to keep the first adventure short, and headed back to the ranch after a mere 30 minutes. Joe was pleased—she'd be all right, this one. Better than all right.

The next day, Joe saddled her up again. This time he decided to pony Peanut alongside, just in case, and go out for a longer time. No telling what might happen. If he got bucked off for any reason, he didn't want to walk home.

The two horses ambled up into the woods, alert and watchful. Curly Girl behaved like a seasoned trail horse, she was so willing. Above them in the afternoon sky, a hawk circled, looking down. The blonde filly looked up and slowed in her tracks, every muscle tense. Joe felt her pause, and halted both horses, searching the sky as well. He saw the graceful bird, flying high above.

Was it…? Could it be? thought Curly Girl, ignoring the rider on her back. That hawk looked so familiar. A shiver ran through her entire body. She shook her head and blinked her big brown eyes, tossing her curly mane.

"Yes, it's me," said the hawk, slicing through the air as it dove closer to the earth. "And I have come from very far away to find you and tell you that your mother sends her love. Regards from Tecumseh, too." Then the great bird dipped and turned and rose again, banking a low curve over their heads. As it flew higher, a tail feather floated to the ground.

"Don't worry, Curly Girl," it called as it climbed into the sky. "Your mother wants you to know she's fine, and always thinking of you. Your mother wants you to be safe."

CHAPTER TWELVE

Homecoming

"Yes, uh huh. That's great. Good news, indeed. Sure, I'll tell her." Jesse looked up from her computer as her mother set the phone down. Her eyes lit up like fire. "Was it him, Mom? Was it?"

"Yes, Jesse. Uncle Joe confirmed that he and Curly Girl should be here by tomorrow! Now finish your homework before you start calling everyone you know."

Jesse clicked her monitor screen closed and ran out the door to her bike. She jumped on the seat and headed straight for Horse Haven. There was the empty stall at the end of her horse's run, just as she'd left it yesterday, the floor mat covered with fresh wood shavings. Armed with a small hammer and nails, she hung up the brass name plate she'd ordered from the feed store and proudly surveyed it, knowing at last there'd be a horse inside to bear its name. Curly Girl, in Colorado, finally!

Looking around the tack room, all the English saddles reminded her that she was the outsider at this particular boarding facility. She never really fit in. Most girls took English riding lessons and wanted to learn to jump. They had parents who drove them everywhere and cheered them on; show mothers and bragging fathers. Well, too bad. She didn't have a horse like those girls, or parents like that, and she never would.

Uncle Joe had loaned her a used Western saddle, the one she was taking such good care of. A brand new saddle pad with green and brown woven stripes jazzed things up a little. Uncle Joe also gave her a Western bridle with silver conchos too, and wonderful leather-laced reins. Beyond that, what else did she need?

I don't need to worry about fitting in, thought Jesse. *I have my horse. My Curly Girl is a real American Mustang and that's all that matters.*

That night Jesse tossed and turned. She could hardly wait for morning to come. Once she finally fell into a deep slumber, she was awakened by a frightful dream. Curly Girl had arrived, and when she stepped out of Uncle Joe's trailer, she was decked out like an English equitation horse with a fancy braided mane and tail, a rhinestone headstall, and wrapped legs. What in the world? She hardly recognized her.

Oh no! thought Jesse, waking up with a start. *This will never happen. I'd never do that to you, Curly. Never. You're a perfectly fine horse just the way you are.*

༄

Jesse's mom called the junior high school the next morning to ask permission to excuse her daughter for an hour so she could meet the trailer at the boarding facility and help her new horse settle in. Uncle Joe was on his way; estimated arrival 8:30 a.m.

Jesse and her mother waited for Uncle Joe and Curly Girl at Horse Haven, armed with carrots, a cell phone camera, and a bucket of new brushes. Jesse was fairly beside herself with excitement.

The Dodge truck with the trailer behind pulled in and circled the parking lot. Uncle Joe stepped out, gave Jesse a hug, and turned to the trailer gate. "Come on," he said. "Be ready to take the lead rope, OK?" He undid the latch, opened the hinged door, and unsnapped the leather strap guard so Curly could back out. But first he reached in for her lead rope, trailed it over her back, and took a good hold.

Curly backed out of the trailer with a jump and snorted noisily. Her brown eyes bulged, showing their whites. Her golden coat was matted and her hind legs soiled in shades of brown and green. Her usually wavy, cream-colored tail looked stiff and stuck together. On top of that, a dull, heavy winter coat had grown in and given her a wild and scruffy appearance. She looked nothing like the pretty golden filly of summer. To Jesse, she looked scared, dirty and miserable. After all, it had been a long ride to yet another strange place alone. She didn't mean to soil herself in the trailer, but in such cramped quarters, it couldn't be helped.

Pulling on the lead rope and raising her head, Curly Girl skittered around, nostrils flaring and tail aloft, a sure sign she wasn't too happy.

"Easy girl. Easy," said Joe, as he handed the lead rope to Jesse. Together they led her toward her stall and the pole-framed run. He unlatched the gate. "There you go, little one."

He'd sure grown fond of this horse.

As he released the lead rope and slipped the halter off, Curly Girl bolted through the gate, practically hitting the rails. Jesse watched through the sides of the run, and waited until she slowed down. Then she offered a carrot, something Curly wasn't too familiar with yet. The horse ignored it and began to pace, whinnying over and over in a high shrill call, as if trying to reach someone far, far away. Finally, she stood in the far corner of her pen and simply pawed the ground, staring off into the distance. Nothing could make her turn around. She was fixed on whatever was out *there*—some other place she wanted to be.

"Oh, no, Uncle Joe," said Jesse, holding back her disappointment. "She doesn't like it here. And it looks like she's forgotten me." Jesse turned away so Joe couldn't see her eyes well up with tears. "What do you think is wrong?"

"She's had a long ride and she's in a new place, hon. No different than you or me. She's just scared. Let's give her some time," said Uncle Joe, putting his arm around Jesse as they walked back to the truck. "Let's give her some time."

CHAPTER THIRTEEN

Breakout

Where am I? wondered Curly Girl. *What is this place?*

The truck and trailer with her humans inside drove away and she was left to take in her new surroundings alone. Someone she didn't know came by to check on her an hour later, threw some grass hay into a manger, and left. The temperature dropped several degrees and a light wind came up; Curly Girl shivered and stood her watch—for what, she wasn't sure. She was hoping to see members of her herd on the other side of the fence, except they weren't there. In fact, no horses roamed freely outside at all, even though the barn was surrounded by pine trees and rolling hills, just like her old home used to be.

As the day wore on, Curly milled about, watching the other horses with mistrusting eyes. Some were turned out in a nearby corral. The barn owner appeared and opened the gate to the run, allowing Curly to join them. Gathered around the feeder, they didn't seem friendly at all. When she tried to talk to them they just snickered at her.

"Who are you?" one of them jeered. "We don't know you. You're a dirty, matted wild thing."

Curly nosed along the ground picking at bits of dead grass and twigs. Not too tasty, but still food. Raised in the wild, she still wasn't used to hay neatly presented in a trough. The other horses continued to mock her while bunches of hay went down their throats.

Discouraged, Curly decided to explore the rest of the boarding area from inside the stall that opened onto her long run. It had a narrow open door that allowed her to get out of the rain or wind. Plus, the stall had a window in the big sliding door that opened into the center aisle. The window had metal bars. From here she could see other horses across the aisle. She looked through it and surveyed the line of stalls. Who or what was that animal in the stall directly across the aisle? It smelled like a horse, but was covered with… all kinds of strange things.

"Who are you?" whinnied Curly Girl.

"I am Belle," the other answered.

"What in the world are you wearing?" asked Curly.

"I'm getting ready for a show." Belle flaunted her bright, lavender-blue blanket and red ear bonnet.

"A what?"

"A horse show, silly. Don't you know anything?"

"No. I guess not." But then, she thought about the honor she had once earned from her own herd, finding the lost horses and returning them, and the promise that one day she would be a lead mare. She'd answered incorrectly. She knew a lot. She knew how to survive. But silly Belle would never understand.

Confused and annoyed, Curly headed back outside. She preferred standing in her run in the cold air where she could see out in all directions and dream of being free. The shelter of pines up the hill beckoned her, as they did when her own herd sought protection from the wind. The

barren pasture, covered with dry grass looked like a good place to roll and scratch her back, but she couldn't do that now. Between her and that field were hard steel rails, fences to keep horses locked up. Most of all, she liked looking up into the sky. The drifting clouds gave her a sense of peace. But not for long.

I don't like this place, Curly decided. *I have to get out of here. I just have to. Why haven't Uncle Joe and Jesse come back? Please come back, and take me away—take me anywhere but here.*

CHAPTER FOURTEEN

On the Road Again

"Don't know what to say, Travis…"

Uncle Joe looked at his watch while his brother continued talking on the other end of the line. It was barely seven o'clock in the morning. Joe had stayed the night at Lynn's house like he used to when Travis and Lynn were together. ("The guest room always has your name on it," Lynn used to say.) Joe had planned to head back to Wyoming and hit the road the day before, right after dropping the horse off, but then thought it best to stay overnight, and see how things went.

"Yeah, well…" Joe continued, "I'm not sure what to think. She sure seemed ready back in Wyoming. Came along real nice; docile, gentle and all. I took her as far as I could—under saddle, on a lead rope too. Seemed to trust people real well, and do her ground work fine. But I went back to the barn last night after dinner with your daughter and dang if that filly wasn't right where we left her yesterday morning, standing at the far end of the run, kinda spooked. Wouldn't come when I called her, wouldn't let me near her, either. It looked like she hadn't touched any food all day."

Uncle Joe took a sip of his coffee and listened while his brother shared his thoughts on the other end. Travis chattered on.

"Yeah, I suppose you're right," said Joe.

"What's he saying Uncle Joe?" asked Jesse. "What?"

"Please don't interrupt, hon. Hey, Travis, hold on here. There's another call coming in. Who could that be at this hour? Maybe I better hang up bro—we'll talk later."

The second Joe put the receiver down, it started to ring. Jesse's mother picked it up. "Nolan residence. Lynn speaking."

"Mrs. Nolan? This is Gail Hall over at Horse Haven. And how are you this morning?"

"I'm fine Gail. What can we do for you?"

Jesse looked up when she heard the name, and her heart stopped as if struck by lightning. She held her breath.

"Well, for one thing, you can remove that horse of yours from our premises, please. That mustang kicked her way out of the barn last night. Broke out one side of the stall while she was at it. She's been running back and forth in the big pasture since midnight, and I'll be honest with you, no one can get near her. I don't have a good roper on my staff here, and she seems real riled up. I'm afraid of her."

"Oh I am *so* sorry, Mrs. Hall," gasped Lynn. "Here Joe; you'd better take the phone."

Jesse's eyes widened. She started to sway. She just knew it had to be something about Curly Girl. Something bad. "Oh please, please…" she prayed under her breath.

"Yes, ma'am. Mornin'. Joe Nolan here. How can I help you?"

"Well sir, I'd appreciate it if you'd come over with your trailer, Mr. Nolan. We can't have a wild horse here at the facility. She's already caused a great deal of damage. Take her anywhere, just out of here. I know how much Jesse was counting on this, but it's not going to work."

"I understand, Mrs. Hall. Apologies. We'll be right over. Please total a list of the damage, whatever we owe you. We'll take care of it." Joe hung up the phone. He looked at Jesse and then her mom, and took a deep breath. His face looked grave, brows furrowed. He put down his cup of coffee and pulled out a chair.

"Let's have a sit-down, Jesse. Time for a powwow, or at least, Plan B."

"What's happening?" asked Jesse, her voice the barest squeak. For her, the world had suddenly stopped.

"Well, it looks like your filly wants life on her own terms," said Joe, "and not be fenced in. Who can blame her? Up at our ranch, we kept her in an enclosure much bigger than what she has at this barn of yours. Sorry Jesse, but conventional boarding will never do. Let me think for a minute. Maybe she can go over to an old friend of mine's place, a cattle ranch some forty miles from here, up in Deckers. You know where that is. She can continue being gentled by some working cowboys and you can see her on weekends."

"Oh no!" said Jesse, "I don't want that! Curly doesn't want that either. I know she doesn't." Jesse's eyes started to tear up and her face grew flushed. This can't be happening. No way.

"Well, maybe, just maybe, your dad could help. He's got the room."

"Are you serious? My dad? *My dad?*"

Joe knew that Jesse had ill feelings toward her father. He wasn't sure what exactly had gone wrong. In part, he knew Jesse faulted Travis for not working things out with Lynn and moving out two years earlier. Father and daughter didn't get along too well back before the split either. Control issues or some such. Travis had a lot to deal with back then and wasn't handling any of it very well. And naturally, when there's trouble at home, kids take sides.

Jesse and her father didn't talk much anymore. In fact, Jesse had been avoiding him as much as possible. But Travis was still her father, and an excellent horseman, a good person, and once upon a time, a very good rancher too. Maybe he could help her now, more than she knew. It seemed like the only solution.

"Board with Dad?" repeated Jesse. "No way. Impossible. I'm not doing that." After all, it was his fault her mother seemed so sad, and at school she had to lie to her friends about her "happy" family, the one she didn't have. Jesse crossed her arms and pouted. "No!"

"Come on, kiddo. The place your father rented in Conifer isn't more than a fifteen-minute bike ride away from here, and sits on quite a few acres. There's a fenced corral. You could get there safely by taking the service road. Beyond those pens is open woodland. Maybe we could clear a path some day for trail riding. It might take a few days with everybody pitching in, but it's worth a shot. Then you could take it real slow and work with Curly as much as you want. Your father is every bit the hand I am, maybe better. Look, I'm going to call him back. You think it over, Jesse, because once Curly is in that trailer we better know where she's going. We don't have a lot of time."

The conversation was over in a few words. "The answer is yes on his side, Jesse. Your dad says bring her over. What do you say?"

Jesse choked back tears, knowing she didn't have another choice. Panic gripped her chest and closed her throat. She could barely form the words.

"OK. OK."

She swallowed her anger and disappointment, and turned to her mother for support. Lynn didn't look too happy. She just shook her head in disbelief while staring straight at Joe, and for once, had absolutely nothing to say.

By eight o'clock sharp they were all back at Horse Haven. Joe walked out into the big pasture, now lightly covered with snow, and headed towards Curly Girl on foot, a long rope in his right hand. As he was about to throw a loop over her head, the horse seemed to recognize him and approached willingly. She came within a few feet and stood still as he slipped the halter on her head and snugged it into place. She even lowered her head and put her nose in his hand. Joe could just imagine hearing her say, "Sorry. This wasn't for me."

Strangest little horse. "What's eating you anyway?" he said out loud as he headed back to the barn. Curly Girl followed meekly, and when they got to the trailer, she stepped right in.

"Jesse, go pick up your tack and let's get out of here," said Joe, looking at his watch. "We've got to get this horse situated and get you on to school."

Jesse scurried into the tack room and stripped her saddle and bridle from their peg. She threw it all into the back of Joe's truck and climbed into the cab next to her uncle. As before, last summer when Curly was stolen, she didn't dare let him see her cry, turning her face away. She could feel the tears starting to fall. But she wanted to cry and scream and pound the door and kick the truck console too! Her heart was breaking, hauling her beloved wild horse away from her very first home in Colorado. Horse Haven turned out to be Horse Hell. How could this have happened? And going over to her dad's? Unreal. She didn't know if she felt sorrier for Curly Girl or herself. It wasn't going to be easy, she decided, for either one of them.

From the back of the trailer came a stomping sound and a wiggle. The trailer rocked on its hitch slightly, then straightened again. Curly Girl centered herself and stood firm as the engine started, the truck engaged, and they all headed out onto the road.

Curly Girl had won. For now.

CHAPTER FIFTEEN

Is this Home?

Travis Nolan had moved into the cabin in Conifer for a lot of reasons. He never thought he'd be there, two years later after signing the lease, still "cooling off." He had things to sort out—losing his job, starting over in another field, problems in his marriage, and more. He'd gotten his real estate license two years earlier when the insurance field didn't go the way he'd hoped, and then decided to sell rural and mountain listings. It sounded so good on paper. He had clients from the Front Range to the Western Slope to southern Colorado, ranch properties mostly. After all, second homes and resort listings were located all over the state. But he never realized how much time he'd be on the road and how long the sales could take.

And then the economy tanked. Listings went on for months, even years. No one was buying. Frustrated customers moved on to local realtors, blaming him for not doing his job. He was treading water in an ocean full of competitors who had local connections. Travis didn't want to admit defeat, especially in front of his family, but maybe he just didn't have what it took to rise above and succeed. Maybe a simple cowboy from Sweetwater County, Wyoming, had taken on too big a challenge.

One thing he knew for sure. Even if he and Lynn were barely speaking, he loved his daughter Jesse more than words could ever express, and he didn't know how to get her back. He and Lynn weren't divorced, just separated, trying to work things out. They tried counseling for a while but he kept missing the sessions. Aggravating his wife was predictable, but how he lost that little girl in the process wasn't anything he ever expected and it hurt.

"Jesse, want to come up and join me this weekend?" he'd ask. "We could go to the Evergreen Rodeo, or catch a movie." Whatever might please her, he offered it. But the answer was always the same.

"No thanks, Dad. I'm busy." And then she'd hang up, like she was afraid of him or something. He couldn't figure it out.

Travis got to thinking about her the summer that he moved out, watching his young daughter one night as she played in her room. Her walls back then were covered with horse movie posters—*Flicka, Spirit of the Cimarron, Hidalgo*—and her bookshelves filled with large and small-scale Breyer horses and colorful My Pretty Ponies. The last time he was in the house, he noticed teen idol rock star posters had been added too. On one hand, Jesse was still a little girl. On the other, she was turning into an independent young woman with her own ideas, her own preferences, and lots of opinions he didn't ever ask for, but got anyway. On top of that, it was obvious that her loyalty was clearly to her mom. But that didn't mean he'd ever stop trying.

Travis's brother Joe in Wyoming had been a godsend, stepping in to help smooth things over, inviting Jesse to spend the last two summers with him and his wife. Their own kids were grown and gone, and they doted on Jesse like a granddaughter, not just their favorite niece. Travis could hardly believe his eyes when Jesse came back in August from her eight weeks on the ranch. How she'd grown, and changed. She'd become a teenager, overnight, and therefore, if he remembered correctly, might be even harder to reach, being in junior high school and having a new peer group, among other things. Could it be that this unexpected situation with the mustang might help move things along? Make things better? He'd do anything for that kid. Anything.

The small two-bedroom house in Conifer, far up in the woods off the main road, had a covered front porch, a stone fireplace in the living room, two bedrooms in the back, a kitchen, one bathroom and a carport. Nothing fancy; perfect for bachelor living. The small living area had a big screen TV, of course, a vinyl leatherette sofa and a small breakfast table with two chairs. It was enough. A guy didn't need much more.

A few animal pens and some low wooden sheds had been built out back. The owner kept farm animals to get a tax write-off. Out front, a wood pole corral held a stack of hay bales and a pen where two spotted goats named Rip and Snort often perched and frolicked, alternately climbing up and down. Keeping them fed and clean was part of the rental deal. Travis enjoyed their antics and didn't mind the extra responsibility. Better than owning a dog. Goats don't seem to get attached.

A split rail fence enclosed the surrounding three-acre site, an area large enough for any horse to stretch its legs and get plenty of exercise. In the front corner of the lot, an aluminum-sided, wood shingled, open shed provided shelter. Not much for warmth, but a structure that could keep any horse out of the wind and snow.

There's no reason at all the little mustang shouldn't feel at home here. She'll be safe and protected. But that phone call from Joe this morning was sure the last thing I expected. What the heck—life is always full of surprises, isn't it? I'm ready to handle this one. Why not?

Joe pulled up to the cabin with Jesse in the passenger seat and guided the truck and trailer into a clearing next to Travis's truck. They came to a stop. This time, when the horse trailer gate was unlatched and swung open, Curly Girl backed out and merely looked around, her head held high. Her ears flicked and swiveled, scanning for new sounds. She smelled the piney scented air and the smoke coming from Travis's cabin.

Nothing to be concerned about here, she decided. The rocky hills and pine trees all around brought back great memories. It was almost like being back in southern Wyoming. *This might work*, she thought to herself. *Just maybe. But where are the other horses? I don't see any horses. I can't be here alone. I need my herd. Nothing else really matters. A horse needs a family to belong to. A horse needs friends.*

∞

The goats bleated a raucous welcome. Curly Girl stood frozen in her tracks.

"Better introduce her to the committee," said Travis with a smile. "Bring her on over, Jesse. She's probably never seen a goat before."

Jesse took the lead rope and led her horse toward the goat pen. Curly approached and snorted, then stopped still. That was a smell she'd never

encountered. The animals bleated something she didn't understand, but it sounded friendly enough.

OK, she thought. *Whatever they are, they could stay. And she would too. For a while, anyway.*

Overhead, a deep layer of clouds had gathered and a November snowstorm brewed in the air. Jesse could feel it coming. "Let's turn her out," said Uncle Joe. "See what happens."

Jesse led Curly Girl to the corral. But just as she was about to release her, a helicopter soared overhead, its noisy roar droning into the sky.

Curly Girl startled and looked up. The giant bird! She panicked, rearing and pivoting onto her hind legs, and then bolted, pulling her lead rope right out of Jesse's hands and nearly knocking Jesse down as she fled. The horse sprinted back out toward the paved road, halter rope trailing behind.

"What the—" Travis caught the end of her rope as she passed him, pulling her up short. "Whoa there you crazy fleabag! Where do you think you're going? Settle down!" he said, jerking the halter rope hard, and flicking the loose end across Curly's chest. The rope left a welt upon her hide. The filly stopped and stood in place, trembling from head to tail, eyeing Travis nervously. She backed up. No one had ever hit her before.

"Hey now," said Joe, turning to his brother. "None of that! I use reward when I train, not punishment. You may have worked horses once, but—I guess it's been a while."

"Yeah, well, maybe it has." Travis answered, embarrassed. "Look, I'm sorry, but this mare seems plum loco if you ask me. She needs some discipline. Is my Jesse really supposed to ride this thing? I thought you said she was ready."

Joe stared at his brother. "Are you suggesting I don't know how to train a mustang? Don't start with me. I know this horse, and I'm telling you she's safe. Why don't you leave the decision up to your daughter?"

Furious over the incident, Jesse glared at her father. She took the lead rope from him and led the horse toward the corral. "Just leave her alone, Dad, would you? And me, too! I can handle her from here. She's afraid, that's all."

Jesse's voice was shaking, as were her hands. She'd never spoken to her father like that before, but she had to now. He needed to know how she felt. This horse was her responsibility, after all, and her problem too. She turned to Curly Girl and gave her a pat on the neck, then went to the gate. "Come on," she said assertively, bolstering her own courage. "You come with me."

She walked the horse through the open gate and around in a big circle three times, slowly, talking softly all the while. Tears flooded her eyes. "Everything's going to be OK, Curly Girl, everything," said Jesse, speaking so only the horse could hear. She hoped it was true. "You'll see. You'll see, Curly. Please don't be afraid."

Jesse's hands still shook so badly she slipped them into her coat pockets to keep anyone from noticing. Besides, the temperature was approaching freezing and she was starting to shiver.

Satisfied her horse had calmed down, she undid the halter and slipped it off. Curly was on her own. Jesse walked over to the hay bales and sat down to see what her horse would do next.

Curly Girl simply followed her to the bales and stood quietly nearby. Nothing more. Then she lowered her head. Nothing could disconnect her from Jesse, apparently the only person or thing that mattered at the moment. As the first snowflakes began to fall, the horse tore into the hay bale and started to eat, pulling out big chunks, as if nothing had happened at all.

"Whew! Well, that's as good a sign as any," said Uncle Joe. "She's relaxed and ready to eat some breakfast. A real good sign."

Turning to Jesse, he added, "You see, sweetheart, nothing to worry about. I think she'll be fine here." Then, checking his watch, he said, "Look at the time, young lady. We better get you to school. I know your dad will be willing to look after your horse until you're out of class, and then we'll all meet back here afterwards to see how things are going. OK?"

"Yes sir," said Jesse, her teeth chattering. She rubbed her fingers through Curly's thick, matted coat and then gave her a big hug around the neck. "Be patient, Curly Girl. Everything's going to be all right. Remember, I love you."

The two brothers looked at each other across the paddock. Their eyes met. A second earlier, a young girl they both adored had just told a wild horse that she loved her. What else mattered? Those words hung in the frosty air like a caress, sincere, endearing words that fulfilled years of yearning.

Travis Nolan understood. He'd loved horses as a kid once, too. Now it was his turn to be a parent, to help nurture his daughter's love for her horse, and more, to nurture something back to life between father and daughter as well. At that moment he wanted so much to give Jesse a hug. But she skipped right past him, and headed for Joe's blue truck.

"I'm ready," she said. "Let's go."

"Your uncle is right," said Travis, as Jesse brushed by him "Now get along. You're already late. I'll keep an eye on Curly as much as I can and I'll see you after school, how's that?"

"Sounds good, Dad! That would be real good." Jesse wasn't sure she believed it but it seemed the right thing to say.

Travis helped Jesse into the cab.

Uncle Joe took the driver's seat. "Uh, hey," said Joe to his brother, "if it's all right with everybody, I think I'll stick around another day or two, OK? I'm sure Lynn won't mind. I'd like to see how things work out. Horse-wise that is. Jesse, I'll pick you up at your mom's house after school and drive you back over here then, fair enough?"

"That would be great. See you around 3:30. I'll be waiting at the door."

Joe nodded. He gestured a thumbs up to his brother and flashed a smile. No time to be in a hurry. Heading home to Wyoming could wait.

As Joe and Jesse drove out of the lot and onto the roadway, Jesse could see Curly Girl standing alone in the middle of the corral, ears pricked forward, eyes wide, watching them go. Even with the windows closed, Jesse was sure she could hear Curly's plaintive whinny as they turned out of sight.

CHAPTER SIXTEEN

Class Report

While Uncle Joe took Highway 73 all the way to Evergreen Junior/Senior High, Jesse pulled out her cell phone in its pink plastic case and opened it to the texting screen. At least a dozen messages from Emma scrolled down its face. They all said something like, "How did it go?" or "Is she here yet?" and "When can I see her?" Then it asked "Where in the world R U and Y aren't U in school yet?"

Jesse texted back with "U won't believe what's happened! Meet me in the lunch room in 30 minutes."

Joe looked away from the road and over at Jesse and smiled. "Can't keep the news under wraps any longer, can you sweetheart?"

"No, I can't. I texted my friend Emma early this morning before you picked me up. I bet by now, the whole school knows my horse arrived. But they all think Curly is at Horse Haven." Suddenly Jesse's face hardened under a clouded expression. Doubt filled her eyes. "What will I tell everyone?"

"What do you mean?" asked Joe. "Tell them the truth. Actually, you can tell them whatever you want, hon. Or not. It's your business, isn't it?"

"Yes, it is Uncle Joe. But, you don't understand…it's like I failed or something…"

Joe didn't answer. She'd have to figure it out on her own.

After Joe dropped Jesse off at school, she practically ran in to the lunchroom. Emma was sitting in front of a loaded lunch tray in the far corner, waving her arms. Jesse threw her backpack on the table and plopped into a chair.

"You absolutely will not believe this!"

"What? What?"

"Curly Girl got thrown out of Horse Haven for being bad and we had to move her somewhere else!"

"What? Oh no! Somewhere else? Like where? What happened?"

"Are you ready?" asked Jesse, putting her hands over her mouth as if she couldn't even say the words, or even retell what happened.

"Yes, tell me already!"

"Being a wild horse, I guess she just didn't want to stay at that barn and so she kicked her way out of her stall and her fenced-in run. Uncle Joe had to catch her in the field. It was a big mess! She broke a lot of stuff. We ended up taking her over to my dad's place because there was nowhere else to go."

"Your dad's place? Are you kidding me? No way!"

"Yes, way!"

Emma, privy to all of Jesse's deepest fears and hopes, knew her best friend didn't get along with her father very well. Who would have ever thought?

"Um, how is that going to work?" Emma asked.

"I don't know exactly. But the best thing is, so far so good. Curly Girl settled right in after we got there. And Dad was cool. Sort of. When I left, Curly was eating and being OK."

"Wait a minute, Jesse. I didn't know your dad had a horse corral where he lives. Uh, where does he live now anyway?"

"Up in Conifer, remember? On Crescent Road. You know, behind the fire station. And I didn't realize he had a corral either."

"Oh yeah, I know where that is. Lucky for Curly. But how exactly is that going to work out? You know…"

Jesse was silent for some seconds, processing the question. She chose to ignore it. "Just like before. I'm going to ride my bike. Only farther, that's how. I have to make it work."

Nothing could stop Jesse now. Not even her feelings about her dad.

"Of course you will. Anyway, it's not that far. Listen—can I see her?" asked Emma. "Can I come over, *today?*" Emma had been just as excited as Jesse for this day to arrive, if not more so. On a scale of one to ten for horse crazy, Emma was at least a twelve.

"Yeah, sure. You gotta' see her. I'm heading back up there right after school with my Uncle Joe. Come! It's OK with me, but maybe you better ask your mom."

"Great! I will. But I'm going with you no matter what. That's all there is to it. Hey! Did you take any pictures?"

Jesse hesitated. The Curly Girl of this morning didn't look anything like the horse in the pictures she had taken in August.

"Um, I did, but—she's kind of a mess. Don't look too close."

Jesse opened her phone to its picture file and showed Emma the few images she managed to capture earlier that day. A broken fence. A dirty rump with a matted tail. And a bedraggled horse standing next to a trailer.

"Oh man, I think she's beautiful!" said Emma. "Are you kidding? Wow!"

"Yeah," Jesse smiled. "You're right. She *is* beautiful. I just need to clean her up a little. Isn't she awesome?"

"Hey," said Emma looking up at the clock on the lunchroom wall, "are you still giving your report in class this afternoon? Mrs. Carlson mentioned it to everyone before recess. They're all looking forward to your presentation on wild horses. Like she said, "Our Jesse is the local expert!"

"Oh my gosh, I almost forgot!" said Jesse, grabbing her backpack. She began to search inside for a folder with some typed pages and photos in it. "Holy cow, I better go over this. Let me get a sandwich or something first. I'm starving."

CHAPTER SEVENTEEN

The Full Report

"And now class, it's time for our weekly report," announced Mrs. Carlson, instructor for the eighth grade Language Arts program. "Our own Jesse Nolan has promised to tell us all about America's wild horses, and I guess everybody knows this lucky girl actually has a mustang as of—today? Isn't that right, Jesse? Would you like to come up and tell us what you've learned? Don't forget, I'll be grading on content *and* presentation, thank you."

"Yes, ma'am, I'm ready." Jesse walked up to the front of the class and laid her folder down on Mrs. Carlson's desk. Then she held up a mounted, 8x10 photo of Curly Girl taken at Uncle Joe's ranch last August, a beautiful head shot with her ivory mane spiraling in the breeze. She put it on the rail of the white erase board.

"This is a picture of my horse, Curly Girl. She just arrived this morning. She's a real wild American Mustang! I wanted to talk about her and wild horses in general because they matter a lot to me. They're the most beautiful animals I can think of in the entire world."

Here, Jesse gave a wistful look at her classmates, as if daring them to think of anything better.

"First, a Curly is a special breed of horse with hair like a poodle, especially in the winter when its coat is thick," Jesse resumed. "Kind of fuzzy, not sleek like most horses. Mine is from the Salt Wells band of wild horses in southwestern Wyoming where horses have been roaming for a very long time. Every year some of them are rounded up and taken off the range. I worked for my Uncle Joe Nolan all last summer and he taught me a lot about them. He helped me adopt Curly, too."

Jesse looked down at her notes. She shifted her weight and straightened her shoulders. She cleared her throat and began again, in a louder voice this time.

"So, to begin with, the word "mustang" is from a Spanish word, *mesteño*, meaning "unclaimed sheep." Later it came to mean a wild or unclaimed horse. I learned that horses came to America by ship with the Spanish conquistadors way back in the 16th century. Lots of them got away though, and became wild. They roamed all over, even to Northern California. Who's seen the movie "*Spirit – Wild Horse of the Cimarron?*"

Several hands went up.

"Well, Spirit was a mustang too. A special kind. Most people say Spanish mustangs are our true American horse, or 'living legends.' I like that description. According to my uncle, we still have wild herds in at least ten Western states, but less and less every year. No one seems to want them on their land."

Jesse looked up from her notes to see if everyone was listening. She blinked hard, trying to look serious. She'd never talked about such an important subject before.

All eyes were on her. She continued. "One of the reasons we still have *any* wild horses at all is thanks to a woman who fought for them —her name was Velma Johnston. She became known as "Wild Horse Annie" because she made wild horse welfare her whole reason for living. In 1950, she was an executive secretary in Reno, Nevada. But because she worked hard to help pass laws to protect wild horses, she became a national hero."

At that, Jesse held up a picture of Velma and showed it to everyone, turning from left to right. "Velma was very brave. She wrote about the roundups, and even tried to free wild horses that were captured! People everywhere admired her, including my favorite writer Marguerite Henry, who wrote *Misty of Chincoteague* and *King of the Wind*, and a lot of other horse stories that I love. She wrote about Velma in her book called *Mustang, Wild Spirit of the West*. Velma believed in respectful treatment of mustangs and burros. She led a grassroots campaign, involving mostly schoolchildren and asked our president to create a law protecting them. In 1959 a law was passed known as the "Wild Horse Annie Act" that did just that! At least it made their capture more humane."

Mrs. Carlson cut in. "You see class, managing wildlife includes horses, too. Isn't that fascinating? Maybe one day one of you might want to start your own campaign about something important, writing to congressmen and legislators. Think about what we can learn here, everyone. Go on. Please continue, Jesse. I'm sorry to interrupt."

Jesse resumed her stance. "Um—it's OK. Velma Johnston was super brave, especially since she had polio as a child and struggled to walk. She continued to protect wild horses even though people threatened her. In 1977, she died, but in the end, she was a fighter, and someone I really look up to. She loved horses and always tried to help them, and that's something to be super proud of."

Suddenly, a hand rose into the air. It was Emma Lee.

"Yes, Emma?" said Mrs. Carlson.

Emma stood up and announced, "I have an autographed copy of the book *Mustang* by Marguerite Henry. It was my grandmother's."

"Thank you, Emma," said Mrs. Carlson, looking at her watch. "Let's save any other comments for afterwards, shall we?"

"Meanwhile," continued Jesse, casting an exasperated look at her friend, "in 1971, another important bill was made into a law. They called it

The Wild Free-Roaming Horses and Burros Act. It was supposed to help protect the herds. It's said that wild horses and burros are actually 'living symbols of the spirit of the West.' I hope you all agree. I know I do."

Jesse's classmates hung on to every word, their solemn faces reflecting their concern.

"Some people believe wild horses are just a nuisance. But one book I read says they are actually native to America. They were here a long, long time ago and belong here. In prehistoric times they were called "Eohippus" and were small, like dogs and later, like ponies, with spreading toes, and lived in the forests. Their fossils are found all over Nebraska, Colorado and Montana, dating from 17 to 11 million years ago. Because of climate and vegetation changes like the Ice Age, they migrated all the way to Africa and Asia where they survived and flourished."

"Who knows how they got there, class?" interrupted Mrs. Carlson again. "Anyone?"

One hand went up, waving wildly. "Over the Bering Strait" came the answer.

Eohippus (dawn horse)

"Very good!" Mrs. Carlson beamed.

"But the point is," said Jesse, "they came back! The author of that book says he can prove it scientifically. "Can I share what I learned?" she asked, taking out a separate page scribbled with notes.

"Go ahead, that's fine. But let's wind it up please."

According to this biologist, our modern horses, zebras and donkeys are survivors of a much bigger group that lived a long time ago called Equus. Equus disappeared and then much later was brought back into the New World in 1519 by a Spanish explorer, Hernando Cortez. The biologist's research proves that today's horse is just like the very last horse in North America prior to extinction!

Jesse stopped momentarily to let her message sink in. This was huge. She wanted people to understand why horses had to be protected. They belonged here. Yet, in spite of herself, her thoughts had begun to drift. She couldn't focus. The difficult, chaotic morning where she and her horse were kicked out of a place she'd grown to love, and then Curly Girl's parting whinny were starting to take their toll. She thought about how lonely her horse looked in that big open pen all by herself and how sad, too. Jesse couldn't wait to get back and be with her. Curly Girl needed some company. She needed a friend. Besides, Jesse was worried that something else unexpected and awful might happen. She hoped her father stayed home to keep watch.

"So," she returned to her report, "horses belong to our country and our state as much as any wild animal, like deer or elk or mountain lions," Jesse explained. "But because some of them have been tamed, some people think they're just one more form of livestock, like cows. The big problem is, we have too many horses and not enough space for them, so every year a lot are rounded up and taken across the borders to be used as pet food." Jesse swallowed hard and blinked her eyes.

Her classmates stared back in silence, their faces grim.

In seconds, a dark cloud had gathered, the presentation taking a somber turn.

"Not more than five minutes, remember?" interrupted Mrs. Carlson, sensing an uneasy shift in the subject matter. She didn't like where this was going.

"OK. Just this last part, please? I want to tell you about a famous wild horse," Jesse begged. But she kept thinking how close her own precious Curly had come to being a victim in that run-down truck bound for who knows where; all those poor animals sweltering inside on that terrifying day when Curly Girl was stolen, and then, that old, scarred gray horse jumping out of the truck and running away. That was something!

Jesse knew she'd never forget that moment, or ever see anything like it again. It frightened her and made her heart pound at the same time. So did rescuing Curly the way they did, and hauling her off in a hurry to Joe's ranch where she could be safe and protected.

As she stood before the class, Jesse could feel a huge well of emotion taking over. Her voice quivered. Her hands shook. She tried to clear her throat. The entire, long course of events culminating in the unexpected chaos of this morning had finally caught up with her, all of it, more than she could handle. But she looked up at the clock and took a deep breath, determined to go on.

"So, back in the 1940s wild horses were rounded up in Wyoming's Red Desert. People hunted them and sold them for profit. But one great horse, a palomino, always got away until finally, he got caught. On that day, a picture was taken of him. They called him Desert Dust and here he is, standing against a big red rock." Jesse had managed to print out a copy of the image on her computer and held it up for all to see.

"That photo made him famous and he was spared the awful fate of so many other captured horses. He went on to become a popular rodeo celebrity and had fans all over the world, making people care a lot about

America's wild herds. I believe we should *all* care about them, and about preserving our country's wild and natural resources as well. That's about it. The end."

By now, Jesse was so choked up she could hardly say another word. She just stared at her friends, and back to Mrs. Carlson, waiting for something to happen.

It did. The entire class erupted in applause.

"Excellent job, Miss Nolan! Well done," said Mrs. Carlson. "You may return to your seat. I think we might just have to nickname you "Wild Horse Jesse!" How does that sound? Any questions, anyone?"

Before any hands could go up, Jesse turned to her teacher, tears streaming down her face. "I'm sorry, Mrs. Carlson," Jesse barely whispered. "Do you mind if I don't sit down right now, or answer any questions? May I be excused for a minute, please?"

I need to be any place but here, thought Jesse. *Wish I was at my dad's place already. Hang on, Curly Girl, I'm coming. I'm coming to be with you, I promise. Just wait 'til three o'clock, OK? My poor little mustang. Please know that I'll be there!*

"Oh my," said Mrs. Carlson, reaching across her desk for a box of tissues as Jesse turned toward the door. "Of course you may. But hurry back."

CHAPTER EIGHTEEN

One Step at a Time

"Jesse, do you think your dad would take on a boarder?" Emma asked. The girls sat next to each other on the front seat of the school bus that would soon drop them off near Jesse's house.

Jesse wasn't sure she heard right. "What? Why do you ask?"

"Cause I am thinking I want to own a horse too and I'll need some place to keep it. That talk you gave today—wow. That really hit home, Jesse, although I don't think my parents would ever buy me a wild horse like Curly Girl right off the bat. I can't ride as well as you, and I don't know all that much about horses either. But maybe they would lease one for me that's already trained and gentled, and I could take lessons somewhere, and then I could board at your dad's too and we could ride together and I could learn even more. Wouldn't that be cool? We could be the Mustang Girls!"

"Really, Emma? Are you serious? That sounds awesome. What a great idea! Do you think there's any chance?"

"Well, maybe not right away, but I'm going to be thirteen in four months and two days, and my grandparents told me I should tell them what I want. It might be more money than they were thinking, but they've been hinting at something big. Maybe a computer or something, but this is what I want. Besides, I've been saving my allowance for years—all those weekends babysitting! And if I promised to take extra good care of the horse, and get a job like you did, well, just maybe. It kind of depends on how much it would cost to keep, I guess. I really want to have a horse like you have."

"I'd have to ask my dad," answered Jesse, a sense of doubt creeping into her voice. "And I'd hate to ask him anything right now. Know what I mean? Like, it might be too soon. Too many things at once."

This morning's unfortunate dust-up with her father and Curly Girl came back to haunt her. "But adding another horse couldn't be that much more work, I guess. You'd have to help clean up after it, I'm sure of that."

"Of course I would. That's our job. We could take turns cleaning up after both of them. But then you and I could ride together, and the horses could become friends and you wouldn't have to go away next summer, Jesse. You could stay here and have fun with me."

"Go away?" Jesse hadn't thought about next summer. Of course she wouldn't be going away. She'd have to face things at home, whatever they were, but now it would be so much easier because she had a horse to take care of and a place to be and something amazing to do, plus something even more amazing to love.

"Well, your idea sure works for me, Emma. I'd like it if you joined me there. I bet Curly would like it too. But gosh, so many 'ifs.' Where do we start? I'm thinking, let's not ask my dad anything when we get there today, do you mind? I just hope my horse is still around," she added, half-joking.

Jesse laughed, but it wasn't very sincere. Deep inside, the trepidation was real. No, there'd be no talking to her father about any new plans for boarders today. After all, there was no horse in Emma's life yet. It was just a dream. But it sure was a nice idea.

Jesse couldn't wait to get home and see Uncle Joe and drive straight over to see Curly Girl. Uncle Joe had a way of making everything seem all right. Thank goodness he decided to stay a few more days.

CHAPTER NINETEEN

Changing Gears

Travis Nolan looked out the window for the tenth time that day. He settled back in his chair and sipped some coffee from the cup he'd just refilled. It was 3:30 and the horse was still walking around the perimeter of the enclosure, as if looking for an exit. Relentless. He was surprised she didn't wear herself out.

After Jesse left for school that morning, the filly started to pace for an hour or more. Then she followed the rail fence, exploring every corner, until she finally slowed down and ambled over to the goat pen. She stayed there until about noon and then started pacing again. Back and forth, up and down, around the fence line, around and around. Finally, by mid-afternoon, she settled down and stood by the hay bales, nibbling at their corners, just hanging out. Then, a little while ago, she started the pacing all over again.

Something about her isn't right, Travis kept thinking. *She's so anxious. Maybe she's not used to being alone.* He went back to his computer, updating accounts.

Finally, he couldn't stand it any longer. He picked up his cell phone and called Jesse's mother. She was still at work. He hated to bother her at the bank but—this was important. He needed to discuss this whole thing. It felt urgent. After three rings the phone call went to her voice mail. "Lynn Nolan is not available. At the tone, please leave a message."

"Lynn" he said, "it's Travis. We need to talk."

Uncle Joe pulled up with the two girls in the front seat. It was almost four o'clock. They'd stopped at a donut shop on the way over and both girls were covered with powdered sugar. Jesse dusted herself off, pulled out her warm gloves and hat, and zipped up her jacket. Emma bundled up too; it had to be below freezing outside.

"Oh. Oh my gosh, I can hardly stand it," said Emma as she hopped down out of the truck.

Jesse couldn't say a word, she was so overwhelmed with relief at seeing her horse—still there, every inch of her, standing in the paddock.

"Could I ride her now, Uncle Joe?" Jesse asked. "Could we saddle her up?"

"Right now?" Joe answered looking at Jesse, and then at her father who had stepped outside as soon as he saw the truck approach. Fully protected from the cold in a down parka and cap, Travis shrugged his shoulders, a look of disapproval on his face.

"It's freezing out, sweetie. Are you sure?"

"Yes, I'm sure."

"If that's what Jesse wants, let's do it," said Joe.

"I'm not so sure," Travis stopped him. "You know how frisky horses get in cold weather. It's barely 30 degrees. Maybe tomorrow? That might be a better plan. I think it's too cold."

"And I think your daughter said she wants to ride, Travis. So let's do it," Joe replied and headed to the trailer for the gear.

Within minutes, Joe had Curly Girl brushed, cleaned, and saddled up. He slipped the bosal over her head, the laced reins knotted over her neck. He kept the halter on underneath and tied the rope around the horse's neck, just in case. Curly's breath rose around her face in frosty plumes.

"Want a leg up?" he asked Jesse.

"No, I think I can get on myself," she answered. Braced with all the courage she could muster, Jesse reached for the saddle horn, put her left foot in the stirrup, bounced a few times on her right, and then threw her right leg up and over, mounting her very own horse for the very first time, shivering, not from the cold, but from pure excitement. Holy cow! Curly felt so good. She was warm and fuzzy and felt steady and sure.

Curly Girl stood still and expectant. Uncle Joe adjusted the stirrups and retightened the cinch, making sure the saddle was on nice and tight.

"You ready, kiddo?" he asked. "I'm pretty sure your horse is."

"Yes! I'm ready," said Jesse, trembling, scared to death for whatever was next.

Emma watched horse and rider from the side, out of harm's way. Clouds of her own steamy breath made little puffs in the air. She hugged her jacket and stamped her feet in the cold. She could barely believe her eyes. Her best friend, on her own horse, at last.

Jesse squeezed Curly Girl with both calves and a light touch of her heels, adding a small cluck-cluck. Curly Girl moved forward, as polite and obedient as any horse could be. Two passes around the big pen at a nice jog trot went without a hitch, without any balking, jumping or pulling. Success!

Jesse turned to her father and uncle, beaming. "We did it!" she said. She petted Curly on the neck. "Good girl!"

"You sure did," said Uncle Joe, smiling. "I think she's all yours from here on out."

"You'd better come in now, Jesse," said her father, heaving a sigh of relief. He'd been holding his breath the entire time. "In case you haven't noticed, it's snowing."

"I know, Dad. I know. But wasn't she great? Wasn't she?"

Emma grabbed a hold of Jesse once she dismounted and gave her a big hug. "You're so awesome!" The hug startled Curly who backed up and tossed her head. "You too, golden girl," Emma said, rubbing her neck. "Just amazing."

"OK everybody, let's get her tack off and give her some feed," said Joe. "That's enough activity for tonight."

"I've got hot chocolate in the kitchen for you girls before you head home," said Travis. "Let's get inside. And hey, Jesse, you were right about this morning. I owe you an apology. I was too rough on her. I think your horse just got scared."

CHAPTER TWENTY

Working It Out

It was Saturday. Curly had been at her new corral for all of three days. By this time, Travis had stopped leaving messages and instead, called his wife at home. She picked up the phone right away.

"I just don't know," said Travis.

Lynn listened and continued to put away the dishes, using the speaker phone. "You don't know what, Travis?"

"What we're doing here. With this wild horse, I mean. Are we doing the right thing? Being responsible parents? That animal nearly killed Jesse the other day. I've watched her bridle, saddle and ride her, and the horse is quiet enough most of the time, but something triggers a panic attack now and then. In fact, she reared and bolted that first morning when she was being led into the pen. You should have seen it. Jesse barely got out of the way. Then again, she went nuts yesterday when a delivery truck dumped a load of firewood out back. Boom! She just exploded. I'm glad Jesse wasn't on her. Who knows when it might happen again? I'm not about to let Jesse risk her life with an animal that's so unpredictable."

"Well then, help her out," Lynn said. "Work with her. Work with the horse. Be around. Keep an eye on Jesse, because she's not giving that horse up. I can see how they've bonded. It's not too late to be the friend your daughter always needed."

"Whoa!" Travis hesitated before answering. He took a deep breath. "OK. I suppose you're right."

"Look," Lynn continued, "I've never seen Jesse want anything so much, or work so hard at keeping it. She's at the corral from the minute school lets out until after sundown. Then she watches training videos, night after night. She gave up most of her babysitting job since she has no expenses except feed, thanks to you. All her time is spent with that horse. I've watched her ride. It's remarkable. She's fearless. And the little mare seems to trust her. But still, I know what you mean. Any loud noise and, even according to Jesse, she goes haywire. But so far, our daughter hasn't been hurt. Let's hope it stays that way."

"OK. Maybe you're right. I shouldn't worry. I'll try to spend more time at the cabin and less on the road. I don't want her being alone with that horse anyway. But I also don't want to intrude on their relationship, training-wise. Frankly, it's almost magical, watching her work with that filly. But if she needs help, I think I need her to ask me to help her, don't you agree?"

"That makes sense. My, my Mr. Travis Nolan, I'm glad to see you're being so sensitive for a change. Here's a thought. Maybe you ought to bring a companion horse in. That might settle the filly down and give her a sense of security. You could ride, too. Ever think of that? You used to be quite the cowboy. Oh, wait, there I go again, trying to fix everything."

"No, you're right. Those are all great ideas. Don't apologize. That's why I'm calling you."

"Well, I swore I'd stop making all the decisions. I agree she needs to be safe. We got into this together, and yet, that's about as far as I can go. You do what you want. You always have. I don't want to argue. But trust me—this is your last chance before Jesse grows up and heads off to college. Growing up happens almost overnight. Be the dad you never were, won't you? Let this horse prove you love her as much as you say you do."

"Lynn…" Travis's voice softened. "I'm sorry. I'm sorry I wasn't around when I needed to be."

"Too late for sorry," she brushed him off. "Make it up to her, not me."

CHAPTER TWENTY ONE

Wanderlust

A week passed and Jesse could see and feel the progress. She wasn't so sure it would happen when she said goodbye to Uncle Joe a few days after the move. He felt satisfied that Curly was in a safe place by then, and that his brother could take over. He reassured Jesse that the time had come for her to take charge of her horse. He needed to head home to Wyoming.

"You just go real slow now, and don' t push her too hard," Joe said. "She'll come around more and more as she learns to trust you."

"I know, Uncle Joe," replied Jesse. "I'm sure you're right. I'll try to do everything you taught me. Thanks. Thanks for everything."

Jesse threw her arms around her uncle and gave him a farewell hug. As usual, she didn't want him to see her cry.

∽

With patience and love, Jesse persevered. She walked Curly on a lead rope and groomed her thick winter coat, carefully combing out her tail. Each day brought new delights. In just a few days, Curly Girl began to respond to Jesse. She came over to the gate right away when she was called, stood while being saddled, and let her human mount up and ride around the fenced area with no difficulty.

Jesse loved her mustang's easy, swaying walk and wonderful slow-paced jog. She hadn't the courage to ask for a canter yet, but it would come. The horse seemed to love attention, and eagerly searched for the fresh carrots and treats that Jesse always had in her pockets. Every single day brought them closer together, each afternoon more perfect than the last. Finally, Jesse Nolan had a real mustang, the ideal, or almost ideal horse of her own.

Sometimes Jesse would look up and see her father staring out the window, watching her ride. Some afternoons, he'd make hot chocolate or cider and have it waiting when she arrived. He'd stop whatever he was doing and talk to her about how school went that day and how well she was doing with her horse. Just like old times. It felt good. He said he liked her style in the saddle and was so very proud of her. He also said she rode like a pro. He was even super nice to Emma, who had the courage to ask him herself if she could bring a horse there someday.

"Sure," he said. "Why not? Whenever you're ready."

∞

Where did my little girl go? thought Travis, watching Jesse ride. Each day since Curly arrived seemed to be better than the day before. Things were going well. The weather had even warmed up.

Seriously, how did she grow up so fast? When she left for Wyoming last summer she was just a kid. Now look at her.

Jesse's newfound independence was impressive. Travis learned he needed to stand back and simply let his daughter be herself, win or lose.

Most nights after Curly was brushed and put away, he loaded Jesse's bike into the truck and gave her a ride home; after all, the days were short and the evenings dark and cold. It gave him and Jesse time to talk and be together. He could feel the fragile strands of trust knitting their friendship back together.

He wouldn't push; he'd just let things take their course. Best of all, he promised Jesse that he'd check on Curly Girl every single night, making sure the tank had water in it, and filling her manger for the last feeding, things his daughter didn't have time to do. He discovered he actually enjoyed it.

☙

I guess things could have been worse, thought Jesse. *Dad's not telling me what to do. He's not being critical or asking me about my social life. He's being nice. Really nice. I wish I had some friends to ride with, but for now, just having Emma around is enough. Dad likes it when she's here so that I'm not alone. Maybe by summer I'll meet some other kids nearby who ride, too. Most of all, I just want Dad to know I can handle things on my own.*

☙

Curly Girl seemed to thrive, adjusting to her environment. By day, she watched the goats at play and munched through her ration of hay. In the afternoons, she looked forward to her young human's arrival, waiting for her by the gate. But in the nighttime, she dreamed of her former life with the Salt Wells band. She never realized how miraculous it was that her herd had survived at all over such a very long time, subsisting in the winters on dry grass, pawed from beneath the winter snow, ever on the lookout for mountain lions and other beasts of prey. Those hardy horses that made it through the winters and gave birth to a new generation each spring carried on the traits of the finest and the fittest. Curly Girl was one of these, a daughter of survivors, beautiful and strong, and born to be free.

☙

Curly stood in the chilly night air, frosty steam coming from her nostrils. She couldn't rest, pacing the enclosure as usual. The two goats had long sought shelter in their shed and were fast asleep. In the quiet, Curly Girl was lonely, young and wistful, yearning for companionship, someone to talk to.

The forest around her lay deep, dark and still, tall trees lit by a rising moon and brilliant stars. A light dusting of snow added a glistening to the pines. Curly Girl pricked her ears, listening, always listening—for what she wasn't sure, but as usual, she only heard the wind whispering through the trees or the occasional hoot of an owl. Some nights she heard the coyotes howl far away, or maybe they were wolves, she wasn't sure. She raised her head and studied the stars, twinkling far away. She whinnied, a desperate lonely cry.

Could it be that maybe I'm actually close to home, to the place where my herd roams? I have no way of knowing from here. Maybe I'm lost like Rocky and the bachelor stallions were and all I have to do is find my way. I do like my human a lot, especially her treats. She's so good to me. She comes to see me every single day. I like the way she brushes me and pets my nose. I even like the feel of the saddle on my back. But at times like this, when the memories come, tumbling like our river in the spring—those golden days in the sun, frolicking with the wild ones—our special meadow where we played, with all our friends, I feel so sad. If only I could get out, maybe I could find them. If only I could get out.

CHAPTER TWENTY TWO

The Next Challenge

Jesse didn't have the courage to trail ride Curly Girl outside of the corral. For one thing, she wasn't familiar with the area beyond her dad's cabin, and for another, he wouldn't allow it. The mountain beckoned her, but the hillside was rocky and covered with dead trees and stumps. An unpaved mountain road wove in and out below, leading to residences hidden in the woods. Traffic there was uneven, and with several blind curves, it was often hard to see.

Travis told Jesse to stay off the paved road for sure. The horse might spook at something unexpected. Plus, it was not uncommon to see elk and deer in these parts. They might appear from behind the trees in front of a horse and scare it as well. A rider could get hurt so easily.

No, if Jesse wanted to trail ride at all, she first needed to explore the area on her own to make sure there was good footing and a marked trail before risking her horse's safety and her own.

∞

Travis suggested clearing a three-foot-wide path down to an open meadow, not more than a quarter mile away. The meadow had good southern exposure, and winter snow melted quickly, making it a good place to ride to and get some exercise. Jesse loved the idea. So, on the second weekend after Curly Girl's arrival, Jesse, Travis, and Emma spent the better part of Saturday creating a trail from Curly's corral gate down through the woods, up and across, and eventually back around in a wide circle from higher ground. The girls each had shovels, wore heavy gloves, protective boots and parkas. Travis carried a small handsaw and a large pick, plus yards of rope.

Emma's mom dropped the girls off at nine in the morning, and by early afternoon the three of them had created a clear path, removed all the sharp rocks, and ended up back at the corral, exhausted but encouraged. "We did it!" said Jesse, beaming. "It looks wonderful. It's good for hiking too. Maybe Mom will want to come. Thanks, Dad. Thanks a lot!"

Jesse spontaneously gave her father a hug, the first one in two long years.

∞

Curly Girl stood at the enclosure fence and watched with interest as her humans came and went. *What in the world were they doing out there?* She could hear them and smell them. When they headed off earlier in the morning into the woods, she whinnied after them for some time.

"It's as if she wants to come too," said Jesse.

"I know," said Emma, who had by this time become Jesse's devoted saddle pal. She couldn't get enough of Jesse and her horse. "Listen to her. It's so cool. She's talking to us! You're so lucky. You have a talking horse!"

Lynn Nolan had driven over by midday and made lunch for everyone in Travis's kitchen while he and the girls were at work. It was the first time she'd been in Travis's place since the break-up and she tried hard not to look at the spartan way her husband lived—the sheer lack of comfort and style. Travis—the guy for whom appearances always counted so much. What happened there? It bothered her to think of him that way. He was so different than that. So different. At least the place was clean. He was always good about picking up.

Instead, she focused on the feast she'd prepared for all of them—a crock-pot full of Jesse's favorite beef chili, a pan of creamy homemade corn bread, a thermos of lemonade and brownies. Mostly, she did it for Jesse. Her daughter was so excited after all, to be able to take things a step further. The making of a trail, a really important step.

෴

Curly Girl watched carefully as her humans went in and out all day. She noticed how the wire collar slipped over the gate post to hold the gate closed. Up and down. Down and up. She'd never noticed that before. It didn't look too difficult to maneuver, even for a horse.

She could see the trail they'd cleared too, as if she'd made it herself, not unlike the many trails her herd had worn up and down their mountain to get to water and good grass, not so long ago. She stood at the gate for many hours that afternoon thinking. *What if, what if…?* She looked at the new path disappearing into the pines. It called to her.

I wonder where the new trail leads?

෴

Jesse and Emma rode home with Lynn after lunch. The temperature had dropped again and it was way too cold to be outside. Earlier that week, Jesse had ordered a map of Conifer and nearby Evergreen from the state geological office and found it in the mail when she got home. Perfect! She decided to study it and plot a real trail system in her father's neighborhood. She might need a permit to do so, that is to go farther than the trail they'd created on her father's rental property, but she couldn't imagine why anyone would mind.

"Let me help you," said Emma. "If we show them how serious we are, maybe other riders in the area would help create it with us."

"Wow! That's a great idea," assured Jesse, thrilled that things were beginning to come together. "We could start a riding club!" For Jesse, it wasn't the joy of just having a horse, but having a good friend like Emma, and even having a dad who turned out to be patient and kind. Oh, and a loving mom who cooked so well, too.

"Supper's almost ready," called Lynn from the kitchen, rousing the girls from their map. "Would Emma like to join us for dinner and stay over?"

"Would you?" asked Jesse, flopping down on her bed. "Want to stay overnight?"

"Sure!"

The next day was Sunday and Jesse was looking forward to sleeping late and then spending as much time as she could with her horse. She wanted her mom to come over to Travis's cabin too, and take some new pictures of her riding. Besides Lynn had made a nice cover for Jesse's saddle and they both wanted to make sure it fit. Jesse's gear was stored in her dad's tool shed and even in winter, seemed to get dusty.

"Yeah, I'd love to stay over," said Emma. "I'll give my mom a call. Can we watch a movie after dinner?"

∽

That night when all was quiet and dark and a full moon had risen, lighting up the pines, Curly Girl made up her mind to head home once and for all. She couldn't be separated from her kind any longer. This was it.

I'm going to find my herd and my mother and Tecumseh, no matter what. Her promise to herself gave her courage. She sidled up to the gate and lifted the big wire loop with her teeth, up and over the post. The heavy gate swung inward, into the corral. Curly Girl walked around it and let herself out, heading straight for the woods, following the brand new trail.

She was free.

CHAPTER TWENTY THREE

Closing In

"Girls, it's past ten. Shouldn't you be calling it a night?" Jesse and Emma both sat up. They'd been lying on the sofa with pillows and fleece blankets watching *The Black Stallion* for the third time.

"Sure, Mom," said Jesse. "Emma, you can go first," she said, nodding toward the bathroom. Emma folded the sofa blanket and headed down the hall.

Lynn saw the opportunity she'd been waiting for. "Could we talk for a minute, sweetie?" She sat down next to her daughter.

"Yeah Mom, sure. What's up?"

"I was just wondering how things are going—um, over there. I know you're making progress with your horse. Dad took some terrific videos on his cell phone and emailed them to me. I swear, you look like you've been riding that filly all your life. I can't wait to see you ride her again in person tomorrow. I'll take both you girls over in the morning after breakfast. Meanwhile, your father tells me you're going to let Emma get on Curly's back. Do you think that's a good idea?"

"Well, I'm not real sure. I thought I'd tie Curly Girl up first. And then if Emma feels OK up there, I'd lead Curly around. But only if she feels real comfortable. I figured if I was there, Curly wouldn't get nervous."

"Oh, that makes sense. Just make sure you have Emma's parents' permission. Maybe call them in the morning to be sure, OK? But… that's not what I was asking about, really."

"I know, Mom." Jesse looked at her and smiled. "I know. You want to know how things are going with Dad. Right?"

"Yes, as a matter of fact, I do."

"Hmmm. I think they're going pretty well. He's been really helpful. It's great having him around if I need something, like adjusting my stirrups or lifting a hay bale. He bought a first aid kit for the tack room that used to be his tool shed, and installed an emergency phone in there too, just in case, and showed me what everything in the kit is for. He wants to be sure I can handle a small emergency if he's not around. I feel like he's really looking out for me."

"You took a first aid course in camp once, remember?"

"Yeah, I do, but now I need to know what to do for a horse as well. Oh, and next week he's building a round pen, a smaller enclosure in the big paddock for doing ground work; you know, warming up Curly and lunging her. It's really worked out OK, Mom. I just wish you could be there sometimes, too."

"Well, like I said yesterday, I'll be there for sure tomorrow. Shall I bring lunch again?"

"That would be great. Like what?"

"Let me think about it. Depends on what I have in the house. Maybe we'll make grilled cheese sandwiches in Dad's kitchen, so the sandwiches are nice and hot. I've got some leftover banana cake and some grapes and…"

"Sounds good!"

"Hey, listen honey, I just hope you're happy there, with the way everything worked out."

Lynn took her daughter in her arms. "You know your father loves you just as much as I do, don't you?"

Just then, Emma came out of the john. "Your turn."

"OK," said Jesse. "In a minute." She gave her mother a kiss. "Yes, Mom, I know he does."

∽

It was past eleven when Lynn's phone rang. She muted The Tonight Show and picked up the receiver, concerned. *No one calls this late.*

"Hi. It's me." Travis's voice sounded soft and sultry. "I need to talk."

"Again?" Lynn dropped back onto the pillow. "Everything all right? You have me worried."

"Relax, everything's fine. I've just been thinking. You were right as usual."

"That doesn't sound good," she answered. "I'm never right. Right about what?"

"Oh no, it's *very* good. You know that idea you had about buying another horse? One I could ride? That's exactly what I'm going to do. I'm going to surprise the girls and take them with me tomorrow afternoon. I looked online and found three decent horses for sale within 20 miles of here and we're going to go pick one out and bring it home. End of story. They're all healthy animals and seem to have good histories. It's the right thing to do."

"Congratulations. What made you make up your mind?"

"I know my daughter needs a trail guide. I know her horse needs a companion. And I know I need to get off my duff and admit that I miss being a cowboy. Remember the man you used to know? The man you married? I just wanted you to be the first to be informed."

"Travis, I'm touched. Thanks. Is that really why you called? To tell me all that? It couldn't have waited until tomorrow?"

"No. I really called to tell you that I miss you."

Lynn took a shallow breath and stopped talking. Seconds ticked by.

"Hey, you still there?"

"Yes, I'm still here."

How unexpected. Lynn looked down at the receiver as if it were a UFO. "Did I just hear that?"

"Yes, you did. And I want us to try harder."

"Travis, I've tried my utmost. This time it's up to you."

"I know, I know. I hear you. And I'm working on it. So for now, would you like to go shopping tomorrow? For a horse?"

"Maybe. Maybe yes. Sounds kind of fun."

"Good. Promise me you'll come. And sleep with the angels, OK?"

"OK."

Lynn hung up the phone. She shook her head in disbelief, a smile on her lips. She hadn't heard that phrase in years. He could be so sweet.

CHAPTER TWENTY FOUR

On the Run

Curly Girl began to canter. She picked up speed as she hit the broad meadow and the clearing. The moonlight made it glow. There she opened up, stretched her legs, and ran even faster. At the far side, at the wooded edge of the meadow, she paused, searching for which way to go. She missed the start of the return trail leading up and back to the corral, and skittered instead through the dense trees, searching and searching, breaking branches right and left. She began to whinny.

"It's me," she called out to the darkness. "Pahaska. Remember? Where are you? Where is everybody?" But no answer came. No horses appeared.

I must be going the wrong way, she thought, sniffing the air for an equine scent. *Please, answer me, someone. I need to get home.* Curly Girl whinnied over and over as she ran, working her way down the mountain slope. Stones and gravel slid under her feet. *I have to get to my herd! How far away am I? Where are the others? Where could they have gone?*

After hours of searching in vain, Curly Girl realized she was lost. There were no other horses to be seen. By early dawn, she had run or walked several miles away from Travis's cabin, far from her comfortable shed, and her loving human. She was a young, confused filly, lost in the Colorado Rockies, hungry and thirsty, with neither decent food nor water to be found.

Remembering her time as a warrior with the herd, Curly knew that in the end, she had to find her way back to a place where she felt safe, where she belonged. She had done it once. She could do it again. But now she knew the truth—if she couldn't find her herd, then she had to get back to Jesse. Perhaps the bitter truth would never change; Colorado was her home now, her family of old just a memory. They weren't around here. They would never be here. She could never go back to what was.

Curly continued to walk aimlessly for hours, now driven by hunger and thirst. Just as she plowed through a grove of trees at sunrise, heading in the direction of the brightening sky, she saw a blur of dark

fur ahead. An acrid, foreign smell sent a frantic signal to her brain. She didn't know what it was, but she knew it wasn't good. It was late in the season for bear, but sure enough, there it was! An angry brown bear stood up on its hind legs, almost face-to-face with the young horse.

"Yikes!" whinnied Curly. She reared, pivoting away.

"Grrrrrrr!" the bear growled and swung a long-clawed paw at Curly Girl, raking her shoulder.

"Ouch! That hurt!"

Crimson blood quickly marked the rip lines from the bear's claws, leaving bright stripes on Curly's shoulder. The bear, seeking a place to sleep for the winter, didn't want to be disturbed.

Curly turned and ran the opposite way, leaping down the mountain toward a winding road, nicking her forelegs and scraping her hocks as she went. No matter. Fight or flight! It was time to flee. As she approached the roadway, a huge, noisy truck seemed to come out of nowhere and sped by, loaded with lumber. It rattled and roared as it passed her, spewing diesel fumes.

Not there! Curly Girl paused by the side of the road, uncertain of what to do. That couldn't be the right way. She stepped back into the trees. She waited, realizing once and for all that she had no business being out in this wilderness on her own. She was lost and scared and had no idea which way to go.

CHAPTER TWENTY FIVE

Lost and Found

Jesse lay in her bed and snuggled under the covers. She'd had a wonderful dream about Curly Girl flying like Pegasus and didn't want it to end. That's probably because she asked Curly for a canter yesterday for the first time! The horse responded with a perfect pickup, transitioning from a trot with a gentle touch of her heels into the most perfect floating gait. Curly even had the right lead, starting off with the inside leg first. Jesse, surprised, took a deep breath and sat it easily, rolling in the saddle with each uplifting beat. It was amazing and smooth and not frightening at all. Three times around the pen left her breathless with excitement. She couldn't wait to do it again!

Jesse threw a pillow at Emma who was lying in the twin bed on the other side of the room "Hey, time to wake up!"

It was Sunday and Jesse knew she could spend the whole day with her horse if she wanted to. Or, once at her dad's, she could ride, then go inside and watch TV for a while to warm up, or play a board game or cards with Emma, or whatever, then head back outside to brush or ride Curly Girl some more, whatever she wanted.

From her bedroom, she could smell pancakes cooking in the kitchen. She pulled the covers up, thinking she'd wait until her mom called, savoring a few more minutes in bed.

Emma was already awake, scrolling through the messages on her cell phone. "Oh my gosh!" she said excitedly. "Oh-my-gosh!" She threw the pillow back at Jesse. "Jes-see! You won't believe this. It's happening. It's happening!"

"What, what?" squealed Jesse, sitting up in bed.

"My grandparents emailed me. They said yes! Yes, yes, yes! I get to buy a horse, with their help. Even before my birthday. It's my Christmas present! Yowee! I get a horse, a horse, like you!"

"Wow! That's so great!"

The moment was interrupted by the ring of the telephone on the nightstand. It startled Jesse. She turned over and reached for the receiver. None of her friends ever called her on her parents' number, only on her cell, a phone she got for good behavior just a year earlier. Who would be calling their house at eight o'clock in the morning anyway? She grabbed the phone. "Hello?"

"Hi hon, it's your father. You up?"

"Yeah. I'm up. Hi Dad." Jesse threw off her quilt and sat up, her body tense. Why did he call?

"Listen Jesse," his voice was slow and deliberate. "Don't panic, please, but I have some bad news. It looks like your horse got out."

"Out?" Jesse let out a gasp. "When? How?"

"She opened the gate all by herself and took off sometime last night I guess, unless you left it unlatched, but I could swear I saw you latch it before I took you home. And I didn't open it again, so…"

"Dad! What are you saying? She's out? Like gone? Where? Where?"

Jesse's mom came into the room after hearing the phone ring. She caught the last few words on Jesse's end, then grabbed the receiver.

"Travis, what's going on?" She listened as he repeated the situation, not believing her ears. "Oh, Travis, no!"

"Lynn, the darn thing's just disappeared. I've looked everywhere, but we need help at this point. I can't find her on my own. Her tracks led into the woods. I followed them as far as the clearing and then… nothing."

Jesse started to shriek. "Mom, we have to find her, now! Please! Right now!"

"We'll be right over," said Lynn. "Just as soon as we can. Girls, get dressed. Boots, gloves, layers, something warm!" Lynn put down the phone and hurried to get her coat on, wrap up some pancakes, and start the car.

Lynn, Travis, Jesse and Emma gathered at the cabin and gave a full report to the county patrol officers with pictures of Curly Girl and every detail they could think of. They called a volunteer horse rescue team to come in and canvass the area on horseback, looking for tracks. Two available members said they'd trailer in and be there within the hour, with a sniffer dog as well.

The Sheriff's Department suggested calling a local rescue team with air support, a helicopter used for aerial search, and ask if they shouldn't get it into surveillance.

"That's probably not a good idea," said Jesse. "Curly Girl is afraid of noisy things that fly. Couldn't we just search for her on foot?"

"Depends on how far she went, or if you really want to find her," said the officer. "There's no telling where she is. Apparently, she's been gone for hours, but we'll do our best."

Jesse and Emma hunkered down inside Travis's cabin, per instructions. It was freezing cold outside and nobody wanted the search to end up being for two lost girls either. Lynn insisted they eat some breakfast, even though Jesse swore she couldn't. Somehow a pancake and some hot chocolate went down.

The day dragged on. Jesse couldn't relax, couldn't watch TV. She got up and sat down, searching the view outside the window. No sign anywhere. All she could do was wipe the tears falling down her face and pray for Curly Girl's return.

It was obvious how the horse had gotten out. Who knew she was so clever? At least Jesse didn't have to blame herself for some failure or her father either. It wasn't anybody's fault. Just a bad design. Not every horse could figure that gate latch out, but Curly Girl did. As everyone's nerves grew more taut, Travis finally got on the phone. It was late afternoon and the last resort had to be called into action. He made the call, spoke briefly to an officer, and then turned to his daughter.

"Here's something encouraging. The Sheriff's Department received a report from a driver recently who said he saw a loose horse standing by the road early this morning. That was over five miles from here. Listen hon, your horse would be real easy to spot from the air. If she's anywhere we can see her, it would take a helicopter to do it. I say we go ahead."

Jesse went numb. She nodded her head. "Oh, my poor Curly!"

"Your father is right, Jesse," said Lynn. "It's the only way. Once we get a bead on her whereabouts, then we can send in some horsemen with a rope. Try not to worry. If she runs, let's just hope she runs in a safe direction."

"But what if…?" Jesse began, then stopped, catching herself.

"What if what?" replied her father.

"What if she's really lost? Or dead? What if she's injured and can't get up, or simply chooses to never come back?"

Jesse's face bore all the pain of the unimaginable, a series of grisly endings far more horrific than she could bear.

"You know, sweetie," Travis answered, sitting down next to her and hugging her close. "Sometimes things happen we can't control. We're doing the best we can. You did all you possibly could to give that filly a safe and loving place to live, and we stood by you. You showed us how patient, tough and capable you are, how very adult you can be when things go wrong, and how generous you've become. We're all so proud of you. It's clear you're ready to own a horse and take care of it properly. If something has happened, and Curly Girl is gone for good, which I am sure isn't the case, I promise we'll buy you another horse. How's that?"

Travis looked at Lynn, hoping to get her approval. *Did I say the right thing?*

"Another horse?" asked Jesse, turning to her father in disbelief. "I don't want another horse, Dad. You don't understand. She made me who I am up to this minute. She gave me the courage to do everything I've done. She's the only horse I want." A small sob escaped Jesse's throat. She brushed away a tear. "But thanks anyway."

Lynn stared at Travis. Travis stared back. Their eyes met in silence.

∞

Emma's parents joined the vigil around noon with two hot pizzas and some coffee for Travis and Lynn. As time ticked by, Jesse's mom and Emma's mother hunkered down with the girls, waiting for some news. Together, they all tried to soothe Jesse's broken heart.

"It doesn't seem fair," said Jesse. "Just when things were starting to look up. We were cantering now, and there's a trail to ride! I thought Curly liked it here, I thought she wasn't lonely anymore."

Jesse had no way of knowing about her father's forthcoming companion horse and how much better things were about to be for her and Curly Girl, but she'd have to wait to hear the news. Travis and Lynn decided it would be best to leave that subject alone for now. Under the circumstances, maybe they wouldn't need another horse after all.

"I don't dare bring up the business of another horse today," Travis said to his wife privately. "I mean, what if Curly Girl doesn't come back? Or has been hit by a car? What then?"

"Absolutely," agreed Lynn. "It would hurt way too much. Hold off." She squeezed Travis's hand. "Gosh—I never imagined anything terrible like this could happen."

CHAPTER TWENTY SIX

Guided by Instinct

Curly Girl scrambled back up the mountain searching for the way she'd come. Overhead she could hear the whirring of the giant bird. She'd know that sound anywhere. *Hide! Hide! Anywhere! Just hide!*

She paused and looked for a place where she'd be shielded by the trees. *You won't get me, not now. Not ever. Not if I can help it.*

She started to sweat in fear and then she started to run. Something deep inside told her which way to go, something she often relied on when she couldn't think her way through a problem. It was late afternoon by then. In the dimming light, she forged a new trail, dashing through the trees, heading up the mountain and back, zigzagging toward Travis's place. She had miles and miles to go, and it would be nightfall by the time she made it, if she did, but she'd get there, no matter what. She had to. The outside world was a very scary place.

"Sure sorry to say so, Mr. Nolan," the officer announced around five o'clock. "But the helicopter radioed in and we have to give up the search for today. It's getting dark. Someone's bound to see her though, and call us if she doesn't get in a wreck somewhere first. Maybe she'll mosey over on into somebody's ranch if she sees other horses. They do that, you know. Go where the food is. Keep your fingers crossed."

Jesse sighed. This was not what she wanted to hear. She zipped up her heavy jacket and went out into the empty corral where she noticed the gate. Someone had closed it. *That makes no sense*, thought Jesse. *It has to be open, just in case. It has to be wide open so Curly can run through it if she comes back. Don't grown-ups know anything?*

Travis put on his down vest and followed her out, heading for the haystack. *Might as well fill up Curly's hay manger while I'm here. Do something useful, think positive.* Lynn soon joined him, bundled up against the cold as well, and went to work, side-by-side, with her husband. After filling the manger together, they turned to their daughter, Lynn's arm threaded through her husband's. "Jesse, it's late," said Lynn. "We'd all better go in. It's over for today."

Jesse had stationed herself on the hay bales to wait. Devoted Emma sat dutifully next to her. "What if it isn't over?" asked Jesse.

"What do you mean?" replied Emma.

"What if she just needs more time? What if she's confused and can't find her way? I can't come in yet. I just can't. I know she's out there. Just maybe if I wait long enough, she'll come back to me, because she knows she's safe here. She has to come back."

The sound of the phone ringing in the cabin stopped everyone. Travis rushed over and bolted through the door, Jesse at his heels. "Nolan speaking," he blurted into the receiver. "Who's calling?" He put the call on speaker phone so everyone could hear.

"Mr. Nolan, this is Ralph Wallace from the Sheriff's Department. We got a call not thirty minutes ago from a rancher down in Pine Junction who said he saw a yellow horse heading north off Highway 285. Can't be sure, but it might be that little filly you're lookin' for. We're trying to catch up with her now."

"Did you hear that Dad? It's her! It's got to be her!" Jesse screamed and started jumping up and down like a pogo stick gone wild, hugging her father, then her mother, then Emma, tears spilling down her cheeks. "They're going to catch her, oh I just know they will. They're going to bring her home. Home to us! Where she belongs!"

Travis and Lynn Nolan looked at each other again, and this time, saw in each other's eyes how much their daughter and her horse had given to them. It was true. They had a home again. Right now it might be nothing more than a dusty corral and a shed with two funny looking goats, but that was enough. That wily little horse was hopefully on her way back. And they had come back, too—to each other. All of them. Curly Girl had managed to make them into a family once more.

∞

The family headed back outside and huddled together in the dark. Emma stood close by with her own parents who had arrived to join in the vigil as well. After a few minutes, the two girls headed over to a hay bale and sat down, shivering in the cold. Jesse couldn't help wiping away a few unwelcome tears.

"OK, let's not push our luck," said Travis to his daughter. "Maybe they'll catch her and bring her back by tomorrow, and by daylight, we'll find her right back where she belongs. Or, we'll have to start searching again. For now, I still think we have to call it a night."

Lynn took Jesse's gloved hands and pulled her to her feet.

"No, please," Jesse protested. "Pretty please? I don't mind staying out here. Really I don't," she begged, her teeth chattering and her breath erupting in frosty puffs. She couldn't abandon her post. Not now.

"You must be exhausted, sweetie," cautioned Lynn. "We all are. There's nothing else we can do. You and I have to get home. Your father can wait for her. You have school tomorrow and I have to be at work early, and at this point, we have to leave finding Curly Girl up to the experts. Besides, we're all freezing."

Emma nodded. "Your mom's right about that, Jesse. I'm like—a popsicle. Frozen solid!"

Travis reached for the kerosene lantern he'd hung on a hook on the shed. It had lit their watch since sundown. He held it up high in his hands, sweeping it in a wide arc, hoping to catch some details, anything, as its light flooded the gate and illuminated the nearest trees. A useless gesture. Still, the phone call had given them all a glimmer of hope. That horse had to be out there somewhere.

"Oh, OK. I guess you're right," said Jesse, defeated. "I give up. I only hope Curly forgives me for not being here if she returns."

As mother and daughter turned to go, Jesse stopped. "Wait. Listen!"

Everyone stopped moving. No one made a sound. Emma took Jesse's arm and their eyes met. At first they heard nothing. Then, there it was again. The faint sound of branches breaking. The two girls stared at each other wide-eyed. Could it be?

From far off in the distance came a sound of something crashing through the brush. It grew louder. Then louder still. Suddenly, there was a noisy clattering through the woods. Travis pointed the long flashlight that he'd also brought with them toward the trees, hoping to catch a glimpse of a golden coat. At first nothing, and then—yes! Yes! Not only a flash of gold in the bright light, but even a brilliant gleam, the light bouncing off a horse's bright eye. From a sound to a blur to the distinct pale form of a small horse came Curly Girl, cantering full bore down the brand new trail!

"Look! It's her!" shouted Jesse. "It's really her!"

Curly Girl emerged from the trees and headed toward the open gate. She swung a wide arc around its edge and thundered into the corral. Jesse met her before she got there, almost in her path. The horse pulled up short, recognizing her human, and slid to a stop.

Jesse threw her arms around the filly's head. "You made it, Curly! You came back to me! You came back!"

Jesse and Curly stood together, each nuzzling the other in a moment of bliss. Then Jesse kissed Curly right on the front of her nose. Travis and Lynn stood back in amazement, in awe of what had transpired.

"Well," said Travis, "what do you know? Jesse was right!"

"Thank goodness," said Lynn, tears welling up in her eyes. "You know what they say, a horse can always find its way home." She laid her head on her husband's shoulder and snuggled into the collar of his coat. A sigh of relief took her breath. To her, it was some kind of miracle that their daughter's little filly had come back on her own.

What else could it be? At least this miracle meant that this night they would all sleep well. And just maybe Travis's good news about the companion horse could be shared after all, adding to Jesse's joy. Curly wouldn't be lonely any more after all. Travis could ride, and Emma too. A perfect ending.

Curly Girl bowed her head low so that Jesse could rub her nose and pat her neck. She trembled from exhaustion on shaky legs and wheezed through spent lungs.

I made it! thought Curly Girl, relieved to have found the ranch on her own. *I don't know how, but something old and wise and powerful guided me all the way.*

Standing next to Jesse, she felt a warm rush of feeling like a flood of sunshine enveloping her, inside and out. She was home and home felt good. She nuzzled Jesse again.

Jesse called her by her name, over and over again, thrilled that she could finally let go of those awful thoughts about her horse being lost or hungry or dead. She rubbed Curly's sweaty coat with her gloved hands. Dried blood caked on her hide rubbed off in bloody scabs.

"Oh look, she's been hurt! Something's attacked her. And she's soaking wet. Dad, I think we need a blanket. She'll catch cold! Mom, I bet she's starving. Could you make her a bran mash right away? Emma, can you get me the salve from the shelf and the bag of treats and my halter too—they're all over there."

Jesse barked orders like a doctor in an emergency room, hoping to save a patient. But her patient was already saved. Her horse was lost no more. Smiles on everyone's face warmed the cold winter night as friends and family together welcomed their beloved mustang home.

Thank goodness I made it! said Curly to herself, tossing her head and seeking Jesse's hand again where she knew she'd find a carrot. Jesse didn't let her down. The carrot was crisp and sweet. Curly stood patiently as Emma rubbed her coat to dry her, and Travis gently placed a winter blanket upon her back.

Now I know the truth, thought Curly with a satisfied munch. *I can never go back to my old herd. Those days are gone. And I guess I don't want to, ever again. After all, home isn't only where you live or where you come from. Home is where you're loved. And I am here to stay.*

༄

High in the sky, far above a thankful family reunited by love, a lone bird soared past a bright November moon. Wings spread, it rode a current of chilly air, carrying it aloft. Its piercing eyes, designed to see so well in the dark, took in the scene below and confirmed one worried mare's constant and fervent wish; Curly Girl was safe.

Curly's flaxen-maned mother, still on the loose with her small herd in Wyoming, could rest easy now and focus on survival, assuring that the new life inside her belly would be born strong and sound in the coming spring.

Perhaps another golden foal might enter the world then, and like all of them, face a challenging and uncertain future. As with all wild horses, they could only hope for the best. Some got lucky once in a while, like one small, golden filly who, in exchange for freedom, could count on a true, forever home.

Curly Girl

CORINNE JOY BROWN is a multi-published, award-winning author, magazine editor and freelance writer. Her recent novel, (2016) *Hidden Star,* was a Finalist in the International Latino Literacy Awards, won the Arizona/New Mexico Book Award for historical fiction, and was named a Silver Winner in the Indies/Forward book awards. Corinne is a former horse owner and longtime advocate for preserving America's wild horses. She has written for *Young Rider* magazine, *Horses in Art, Working Ranch* magazine, and *Cowboys n' Indians,* among others. Her first book about horses for young readers, *Wishful Watoosi—The Horse That Wished He Wasn't* is a national favorite. Corinne is committed to teaching the next generation about the power of horses to teach and heal.

GINNY MCDONALD, an award-winning illustrator, is an advocate of wild horses. She is the adopter of an American Curly mare, a distinct breed that can be found in the Wyoming Salt Wells Creek Herd Management Area (HMA) of wild horses, as well as a horse from the Wyoming Divide Basin HMA. Ginny's attention to fine detail using Prismacolor colored pencils to illustrate *Finding Home* is second only to her exquisite draftsmanship, and the ability to portray real emotion, an exceptional talent among illustrators.

CPSIA information can be obtained
at www.ICGtesting.com
Printed in the USA
LVHW022055011020
667644LV00007B/137